Library of
Davidson College

CHATHAM HOUSE ESSAYS: 7

CHANGING PERSPECTIVES
IN BRITISH FOREIGN POLICY

CHATHAM HOUSE ESSAYS

Previous essays in the series have been:

1 *The Chinese View of Their Place in the World.* By C. P. FITZGERALD
2 *The China-India Border: The Origins of the Disputed Boundaries.* By ALASTAIR LAMB
3 *The Debatable Alliance: An Essay in Anglo-American Relations.* By CORAL BELL
4 *Sterling in the Sixties.* By CHRISTOPHER MCMAHON
5 *Ballot Box and Bayonet: People and Government in Emergent Asian Countries.* By HUGH TINKER
6 *Imperial Outpost—Aden: Its Place in British Strategic Policy.* By GILLIAN KING

The Royal Institute of International Affairs is an unofficial body which promotes the scientific study of international questions and does not express opinions of its own. The opinions expressed in this publication are the responsibility of the author.

Foreword

By Michael Howard

THIS essay had its origins in a proposal, made in the autumn of 1963, that discussion should be organized in Chatham House on the problems which face Britain after her attempt to join the European Economic Community and its failure in January 1963. It was suggested that a publication dealing with this subject should be planned to appear if possible early in the lifetime of the new parliament which would result from the general election of 1964.

In view of the controversial nature of the subject and the limited time available, it was thought that a report attempting to represent the consensus of opinion of a Study Group would run the risk of ending as little more than a record of differing points of view and would in any case take too long to produce. It was therefore decided that the publication should be the work of an individual author, after participation in discussions with a Study Group, whose members would not be asked to take responsibility for the opinions expressed in the essay.

Kenneth Younger, the Director of Chatham House, was asked to write the essay, and a Study Group was formed with the following members: Professor Michael Howard (Chairman), Alastair Buchan, Miriam Camps, H. F. R. Catherwood, David Howell, Evan Luard, Roger Morgan, Herbert Nicholas, George Schopflin, Andrew Shonfield, Donald Watt, Shirley Williams, Kenneth Younger. As is usual at Chatham House, the Study Group had the benefit of the presence of members of several government departments who took part in the discussions on a purely personal basis.

The Group met seven times between November 1963 and March 1964 to discuss 'The Changing Framework of British Foreign Policy'. Papers, on topics corresponding approximately to the chapters of the present essay, were submitted to each session. No attempt was made to reach collective conclusions and the finished work, which expresses views often markedly in conflict with those of individual members of the Group, must therefore be regarded as the author's exclusive responsibility.

The Institute and the author wish to express their thanks to the members of the Group for the help and stimulus they have been given in the preparation of this essay.

June 1964

Contents

Foreword, by MICHAEL HOWARD   v

1. Britain after Brussels   1
   - Britain's historic role   2
   - The end of Empire   3
   - Separateness from Europe   4
   - The three circles of policy   7
   - Interdependence   12
   - The decision to be made   14

2. The Cold War and East-West Relations   15
   - The problems of North and South   15
   - The nuclear balance   17
   - Continuing causes of friction   19
   - The 'bipolarization' of power   22
   - The Gaullist 'third force' concept   25
   - China   27

3. The Shape of the Western Alliance   30
   - The Atlantic Alliance   30
   - The American Grand Design   33
   - Possible alternatives   36
   - Britain and the 'two pillars' concept   38
   - The Nassau agreement   41
   - The Mixed-Manned Force   45
   - Collective nuclear defence   46

Contents

4. World Security after the End of Empire	53
British overseas commitments	54
The Middle East and Far East	57
An international security system	67
5. Britain in World Trade	72
The objective of multilateral trade	73
EEC and the Kennedy round	75
EFTA	76
Effects of the Brussels negotiations	78
Britain and the Commonwealth	81
The role of sterling	84
6. The Options Open to Britain	88
Must Britain integrate?	88
Britain and EEC	92
De Gaulle's view of Europe	96
The revival of nationalism	98
European-American relations	100
British influence in Europe	102
The special relationship with the U.S.	107
Relations with the Commonwealth	110
7. Policy for the Future	115
The end of an era	115
The concept of multilateralism	118
The search for international identity	120
The pattern of co-operation	121
Policy towards the EEC	125
Multilateralism in practice	129
A new national purpose	135

I
Britain after Brussels

THE negotiations which took place in Brussels between October 1961 and January 1963 are an obvious taking-off-point for the discussion of Britain's international future. One does not need to agree with the British government's decision in order to appreciate the historic significance of a British attempt to join a continental European Economic Community in a manner clearly requiring a measure of economic integration and, almost equally clearly, implying a willingness to take the first steps towards a common foreign policy with her European neighbours.

Not since the loss of the last English possessions in France had so intimate an identification with the European continent been contemplated. Involvement in Europe's affairs and in most of her wars Britain had not been able to avoid, but she had sought to preserve her interests by various combinations of isolationism and alliances and by manipulating the balance of power among the great states of Europe. Never, if one excepts Churchill's romantic gesture to France in 1940, had a British government thought of handling Britain's European relationships from inside Europe. That she decided to do this in 1961, after so many centuries of aloofness, was the measure of the fundamental changes which had occurred in Britain's situation in the world.

Britain's historic role

These changes had been occurring over a long period. Britain's nineteenth-century pre-eminence in world affairs, though never as great as the nostalgically-minded are inclined nowadays to claim, was nevertheless real, and it lasted at least until 1914. Between the two world wars its basis was much less evident, but the prestige still enjoyed by Britain in many countries and, in the main, her own confidence in herself as a great power, combined to enable her to continue much of her old role in many different parts of the world. The fact that the United States retreated into isolation, while Russia underwent violent revolution and civil war, postponed for a generation the day when Britain would have to re-think her international position in a world of giant continental states.

When the Second World War ended in 1945 the new era could be seen to have arrived. Despite the distinction which Britain had gained by being the only allied power to fight the war from start to finish, the disparity in power between her and the two leading victors, the United States and the Soviet Union, was now beyond argument. Even on the Western European front, the American contribution in men and material far outstripped the British: in the war against Japan the difference was even more marked. Economically, it only needed the abrupt ending of Lend-Lease in the autumn of 1945 to dramatize the extent of British dependence on outside aid.

Yet once again there were factors which, if they no longer concealed Britain's changed circumstances, nevertheless postponed for a further decade the moment when Britain was ready to give her mind effectively to considering what options were open to her. The first of these factors was simply the general chaos in which the world found itself and in particular the virtually total collapse or exhaustion of so many of the former great powers. Even the Soviet Union's ability to affect events outside her own boundaries was virtually limited to Eastern Europe. Indeed the United States was at that time the only true world power. In terms of her world responsibilities, Britain came easily second, and although her power to discharge them might be limited, she nevertheless rightly felt herself to be still the same sort of power that she had been before, handicapped indeed by lack of resources, but still cast for a world part, which no one else, for the time being, could play in her stead.

The end of Empire

The early post-war years saw the transfer of a growing number of Britain's responsibilities to the United States, notably over the occupation of Germany and in the Near East. They also saw the first and decisive stage in the transformation of British imperial responsibilities into the vaguer duties owed to an independent Commonwealth. This process made the economic support of large areas of Asia into an international rather than a purely British concern, thus once again permitting the United States, the only country capable at that time of giving aid on a grand scale, to take some of the burden off British shoulders.

After a brief period around the end of the war, when the United States was momentarily inclined to see the effete British Empire as one of the obstacles to the creation of an up-to-date world order, the wartime American-British alliance settled down once again to a period of effective partnership, based on compulsive common interests. On the one hand Stalinist policies in Europe had, by 1948-9, re-created Anglo-American military solidarity, which might otherwise have dissolved, and Britain was still the only ally of the United States which had any substantial military strength to contribute. On the other hand Britain, having taken the decision to effect a peaceful transfer of power in her Asian and eventually in her African dominions, was fully conscious that only the political, economic and moral support of her powerful ally could enable her to complete this process peacefully, without opening up many poor and vulnerable areas of the world to confusion and subversion.

In the decade after the war, the energies of Britain's foreign policy makers were overwhelmingly devoted to these two tasks, defence in Western Europe and laying the foundation for a new world-wide Commonwealth. For both, intimate American co-operation was indispensable, and for both it was forthcoming. Looking back from the vantage-point of the mid-1960s, one would not wish to change the priorities. Both tasks had to be performed. Britain's role in European defence, though secondary to that of the United States, was important: in the Commonwealth it was indispensable. Indeed if Britain had failed to take the key decision over India in 1947, not only would the Empire almost certainly have wound up in blood and tears, but the winding up of the other European empires, from Indonesia to Algeria, might well have been far more damaging to the West as a whole than, in the event, it was. Mistakes in detail and in execution there may have been, but in broad conception these British policies were right and represented the biggest contribution to world stability that Britain could have made in those years.

Separateness from Europe

Nevertheless these necessary preoccupations served to perpetuate a feature of the British attitude to world affairs which, in the longer run, may seem to have been less far-sighted—the sense of separateness from Europe. The deep historical causes of this feeling, to which reference has already been made, had been accentuated by the physical separation of the war years, when Europe was under hostile control and the friendly reality was the English-speaking world. (The Russians, though deeply admired in Britain during the war, were too remote to arouse an equal feeling of human solidarity.) For some years after the war, most of Europe was in no shape to undertake joint action with Britain for common purposes. Although the organization of post-war defence began with the purely European treaties of Dunkirk and Brussels, the essential objective for Britain was always to involve the United States in European defence, and, when this was effected through NATO, it was the British-American link to which Britain continued to give priority.

This was not a wrong policy in itself, for NATO as a whole undoubtedly depended, as it still does, overwhelmingly upon American support. But an unintentional by-product of the policy was a prolongation of the feeling, both on the continent of Europe and in Britain, that, within the Atlantic Alliance, the Continent was one thing and North America and Britain were another, just as they had been from 1941–5.

Two new developments reinforced this trend. The first was the evolution of nuclear weapons and the American attitude to the sharing of nuclear secrets. Britain, having been refused the post-war co-operation of the United States in nuclear matters and having decided to go on alone, was far ahead of Europe in the development of her own nuclear weapons, and in due course made enough progress to qualify for favourable treatment under American legislation. This, coming on top of the specially favoured position which wartime habit still assured to British service chiefs in Washington, placed Britain increasingly on the American side of the divide, which separated the overwhelmingly powerful Americans from their allies in Europe.

The second new development was the growth of the movement in Western Europe for European unity. Emerging from old historical roots, it achieved a new growth in the early post-war years, because of the breakdown of European national institutions between 1940 and 1945 and the consequent feeling that Europe must organize itself internationally, if it was to avoid tearing itself apart again in further civil wars. Here again was something not shared by Britain, whose national institutions, including Parliament, had emerged from the war triumphantly vindicated. This divergence was further emphasized by the fact that the European figureheads of the post-war movement for European unity were a group of statesmen—Adenauer, De Gasperi, and Robert Schuman—whose ideology was specifically Roman Catholic and their political experience that of men concerned with the borderlands of Latin and German culture, with the Rhineland, the Tirol, and Alsace. While Britons might approve and even applaud a movement for European unity based upon this immediate motivation, it is easy to see that it was something which in their hearts they could not share and to which they felt outsiders.

When the question of Britain's official attitude to Europe first came to the fore, with the Schuman Plan in 1950, it seemed that the existence of a Labour government, with its instinctive distaste for the European Catholic parties, was an aggravating cause of the lack of understanding between Britain and Europe at that stage. But the sequel, in which Conservatives came to power little more than a year later, only to continue Labour's attitude towards Europe, suggests that this circumstance was at best marginal and that the difficulty lay deeper.

The difficulty, in fact, lay less in any ideological distaste on one side or the other, than in the absence of a sufficiently positive sense of common purpose between Britain and her neighbours. Even the common problem of the evolution of their respective empires, so far from providing a bond, caused nothing but suspicion. The European empires died harder than the British, and amid greater bitterness. The resentment felt by the former imperial powers of Europe over the attitude of their allies towards Syria, Indonesia, the Congo, and Algeria had no British parallel, apart from the momentary anti-American spasm in Britain over Suez after 1956. Right up to the moment when President de Gaulle cut the Gordian knot in Algeria, the long process of decolonization tended to make the British feel both different and superior to their European neighbours, while it tended to turn European minds inwards towards their own continent, if only to escape the contemplation of humiliations overseas, for which, in some cases at least, they held the Anglo-Saxons partly to blame. Though it is mainly the American attitude which was resented, Britain cannot complain, in view of her steady pursuit of Anglo-American solidarity, if some of the odium rubbed off on her.

The three circles of policy

With so much ambivalence in the British mind about Britain's future, it is not surprising that British policy during most of the post-war period lacked a single clearly identifiable purpose. For a full ten years after 1945 Britain seemed primarily concerned to keep open as many options as possible. The best description of this policy is still the impressionistic formulation, made by Winston Churchill, of the three overlapping circles: Britain and the Commonwealth, Britain and the United States, and

Britain and Europe. While this formulation did not, of course, claim that Britain was at the centre of each of the three circles, it was nevertheless a self-flattering concept, implying, correctly enough, that Britain was important in all of these three groupings and that she was entitled to be thought of as a member of all three without belonging wholly to any one of them. For ten years or so this three-cornered policy worked well enough, though the quality of the relationship within each of the circles was constantly changing. While it lasted, it had the advantage, always dear to diplomatic practitioners, of extreme flexibility. It could be operated pragmatically from year to year and from issue to issue, the partners in each of the circles being consulted or at least informed, but never having any formal right to a voice in British policies, let alone a right of veto.

That this conveniently non-committal attitude would not be indefinitely sustainable became clear when the European signatories of the Treaty of Rome in 1957 decided that membership of the European Economic Community should involve formal obligations and a progressive merging of sovereignty. Though the form of the treaty was economic, it was no secret that it was intended as a step in the direction of political unity as well. This was epitomized in the statement that no one could expect to join the economic club without paying the political price, and it was on this rock that all British efforts to participate in a free trade area in Europe foundered. By the end of 1958 Britain faced the prospect of exclusion from the European circle, with consequential separation from the markets of the Community by a tariff barrier. Looking farther ahead, there was the prospect that the industrial strength of the Community would make it a formidable competitor to Britain in the markets of the world; while, if it later came to political maturity, the Community might gradually become the first ally of the

United States. Britain also faced the depreciation of her second circle, the relationship with the United States. This was partly because the United States strongly favoured the integration of Europe, preferably with Britain as a member, even at the cost of trade discrimination against herself by the new Europe, but was not disposed to adopt a similar attitude to any purely commercial free trade area which Britain might devise, since this would not offer the promise of political integration, which was what gave the Community its appeal in Washington.

The special nature of Britain's relationship with the United States was by this time coming to be questioned on other grounds as well. The bitterness of the inter-governmental quarrel over the Suez invasion of 1956 had left an undertone of resentment in Conservative circles in Britain and on the American side had planted a new doubt about the time-honoured belief in British sophistication in world affairs. When the Suez crisis was over, the speed with which Macmillan managed to restore good relations with the American administration was the subject of admiring comment. Yet the old relationship could not be restored in its entirety. It had depended to some extent on myth, and, after the smash, Humpty Dumpty could not be put together again. The relations, from that time onwards, had to be founded upon a harder calculation of material resources. On this basis the relative lack of dynamism in the British economy, together with the ever-widening gap between the United States and Britain in nuclear armaments and missile techniques, pointed to a relative devaluation of British influence in Washington, which even the friendliest personal relations could not wholly disguise.

The Suez crisis had less effect upon the remaining circle, the Commonwealth. The incident occurred just before the second phase in the transformation of the Empire began, so that there were no independent Commonwealth governments in Africa other than the Union of South Africa. In view of the violent disagreements that arose, it was accounted a triumph that no Asian country renounced its membership, and that by the time Malaya and Ghana reached independence in the following year, and so became eligible for Commonwealth membership, the dust had settled sufficiently for the whole affair to be ignored. The Commonwealth had thus shown a reassuring capacity for survival, though its capacity to influence events had been less evident.

The effect of the Suez crisis upon Britain was more lasting. It was not only that it had demonstrated that the United States was capable of flatly opposing Britain where important British interests were at stake, and that the new Commonwealth was markedly less susceptible to British leadership than the old. More significant, it had dramatized and made patent, what thoughtful men had long known, that the United Kingdom by herself could no longer claim to be a great power. Unable to rally the Commonwealth, she could be thwarted in a major enterprise simply by a United States refusal to back the pound sterling. Though the first reaction to this unwelcome discovery was merely a howl of frustrated rage, the way had been paved among many conservatively-minded people for the idea that economic union with a group of wealthy European neighbours of roughly her own size might offer Britain a greater reality of independence than her position of vulnerable eminence in the Commonwealth or her junior partnership in an American world. If, as President de Gaulle is said to believe, a Conservative Britain is destined in due course to opt to join Europe on Gaullist terms, it is in the delayed shock arising from the Suez debacle that the origin of such a decision will have to be sought.

In the comparatively brief period between 1956 and

1961, when the British application to join the Treaty of Rome was made, a whole series of events was thus beginning to suggest that Britain would soon have to face difficult choices. Suez, the Rome Treaty, the failure to create a free trade area, new pressures from the Kennedy administration in the United States, the virtual end of the decolonization process and, last but not least, the contrast between bounding production in the Common Market countries and the disappointing showing of the British economy at the time—these all combined to make the government look around for some new and if possible dramatic departure of policy. They also combined to induce in a large part of the British public a reversal of its previous attitude to Europe. From having long felt a sense of superiority over the Continent, based on Britain's overseas connexions, and upon her political stability, this section of opinion jumped, perhaps with undue haste, to an exaggerated belief that Europe had found a politico-economic technique which was already leaving British industry behind and would shortly also bring the vast resources of the Community of Six within a single political authority.

It would be wrong to suggest that this evolution was characteristic of British opinion as a whole. Only briefly in the last months of 1961 did the opinion polls show as much as 50 per cent of the public in favour of joining the European Economic Community and the percentage of undecided voices remained continuously high. Nevertheless the evolution was unmistakable in the Whitehall departments, in the government itself, and in business. Here the problem was discussed largely in economic terms and, as the moment of decision approached, it was on the economic plane that the argument was presented to the public. In view of the timetable by which the government hoped to lead the country into Europe before the election of 1964, it may be that a full discussion of the political issues would not have been practicable and that the government was taking no more than a legitimate gamble in hoping to bring the economic negotiations with Europe to a conclusion first and to sort out the political implications at leisure afterwards. However that may be, it was doubt about the political rather than the economic aspects which kept British opinion divided, and it was the consequent uncertainty in Europe about the firmness of British political intentions which eventually gave President de Gaulle his cue for bringing the British initiative to a halt.

Interdependence

The truth is that what is now at stake is the shape of the world, or at least of the Western world, after the dissolution of the European empires, including the British. There could scarcely be a bigger political issue than that. The dissolution of empire is usually a painful and violent process involving the collapse of the imperial power. This has not happened to any of the imperial powers of Europe since 1945. Britain's experience has been the most untypical of all, because the loss of imperial power has involved her in almost no violence, and the process has been comfortably cushioned for her, morally by the transformation of Empire into Commonwealth, and materially by the wave of affluence on which the British people at home have been carried along, together with the rest of the Western world. Neither the older imperialists nor their Marxist opponents would have believed that the end of Empire could be so painlessly achieved.

For all this there is cause to be thankful, but the very absence of melodrama carries with it the risk that a decline in British power and in purpose may be too passively accepted, because the fundamental nature of the change has not been appreciated, or has been made tolerable by illusions which are liable later to fade. As a heavily populated, industrialized nation, dependent for her existence upon international trade and for her security upon the support of other powers, Britain cannot simply retreat into her shell. In the past she has influenced world events by methods which are now becoming obsolete. She now has to find new means for achieving similar ends. For her, international interdependence is not so much an aim which she can choose as a condition of her existence.

Interdependence may take many forms, and one of the questions which the Brussels negotiations brought to the forefront of the British consciousness was whether, for Britain, it must take the form of economic and eventually political integration into a larger unit, capable of matching the great new continental nations. This question is an agonizing one for Britain, because, if it be answered in the affirmative, Britain has no choice but Europe, since integration into either of the other two circles of British postwar policy is not a possibility. More than this, it is not even sure that she could now secure integration with Europe if she sought it.

The abrupt termination of the Brussels negotiations virtually ruled out any immediate British initiative, and the imminence of British elections postponed the opening of the next phase at least until late in 1964. Nevertheless events do not stand still, either in Europe or elsewhere, and if Britain were simply to abstain from taking initiatives for a more or less prolonged period, she would be likely to find that her future had been determined for her. The debate following the election will be concerned with the question whether Britain can command her fate, or whether she must be content merely to acquiesce in it, whatever it may turn out to be.

The decision to be made

There are several ways in which the issues of which this debate is made up might be approached. The approach to the Brussels negotiations was economic and it might be argued that an analysis of British economic interests is the logical starting-point for any fresh discussion. On the other hand, as has already been noted, it was the political and strategic implications of Britain's relations with Europe which, in the end, came to absorb attention and were the immediate reasons for the breakdown.

So, now, it seems that politics and strategy are the fields in which most is at stake. Economically a technically advanced country such as Britain can probably earn an adequate living within any of the alternative frameworks of world trade which are likely to develop. What she has to decide is rather the way in which she can best make her influence felt in the great issues of war and peace, and in the problems of organizing collective security and promoting international stability in an age where the peace is no longer kept by imperial powers. She has also to find a new identity for the British community in a world where no one can be 'an island unto himself', but where the mechanisms of a new global order either do not exist at all or are still in the feeble stage of infancy. It is with these questions, none of which can be sharply separated from the need for Britain to be economically and commercially buoyant, that the remainder of this essay will be concerned.

2
The Cold War and East-West Relations

EVER since the late 1940s the international policies of the major powers have been dominated by the problem of East-West relations and by the tensions compendiously described as 'the Cold War'. Though large areas of the world have protested that this problem is not their central problem and have proclaimed their refusal to align themselves with either of the two contesting blocs, nevertheless, in the centres where military and industrial power lie, the Cold War has taken precedence over all other issues.

The Problems of North and South

It is true that, particularly in the last few years, influential voices have been heard to say that an even more fundamental question is that of the relations between North and South, between the 'developed' and the 'developing' continents. In the long run this may well be true, in the sense that the gulf between areas of the world which are at different stages of their social and technological evolution may prove to be more significant and harder to bridge than the current ideological differences which separate some developed countries from others. One cannot quarrel with the attempt to place a higher valuation upon the challenge offered by the less developed areas of the world. But the first condition of this challenge being met at all by those countries which have the resources and skills required is that no major nuclear war is allowed to break out, that tensions such as those over Berlin or Cuba are kept under control and, preferably, that some measure of disarmament or at least control of the arms race is secured. Unless in the short run these things can be achieved in the context of East and West, there will be no long run in which to solve the problems of North and South.

The tensions which grew up between the Soviet Union and the Western powers after the end of the Second World War gave to the East-West conflict an ideological quality which, ever since, has made it hard for the two sides to treat each other objectively and, in particular, to allow their attitudes to alter as the conditions of the conflict changed. On the Soviet side Khrushchev has felt obliged to accompany every move which he has made towards a normalization of East-West relations—and he has made a good many—by a firm reaffirmation of his ideological position and an assertion that coexistence means no more than a sensible agreement not to attempt to settle the ideological battle by the use of modern weapons of mass destruction. The corresponding attitude in the West is typified by those, mainly in the United States, who see East-West relations in simple black and white, as a struggle between good and evil in which the good can prevail only by the total defeat of the bad.

This Western attitude is much less prevalent today than it was, and, among Western governments it is now widely accepted that real changes have been occurring in the communist world, requiring changed reactions from the West. It is the nature and extent of these changes which now have to be assessed, and on this no effective consensus has yet emerged.

The nuclear balance

The principal cause of the change in the relations between the blocs is the evolution of nuclear armaments and strategy. From the time when American-Soviet discussions were resumed after the abortive Summit Meeting of 1960, it became increasingly evident that both the United States and the Soviet Union had begun to recognize their common interest in the avoidance of nuclear war. So generally was this accepted that the Soviet government's action, in the autumn of 1962, in installing rocket bases in Cuba, was at first greeted with incredulity as well as alarm, and when the full truth was established, it made the trend which had been developing seem a fraud. But once the crisis was past, and the Soviet adventure was seen to have bought little or no results at the price of very considerable risks, the net result was that the former trend was reinforced. The two great nuclear powers had seen the whites of one another's eyes and had concluded that they did not wish to repeat the experience.

That the Cuban crisis was followed by a lessening of tension and a reduced fear of major war is undeniable. At the same time it demonstrated the precarious nature of the strategic balance and the risk of deception which is still involved in any simple acceptance of a superficial lessening of tension, unless there is also genuine progress towards agreement on disputed issues. So the feeling that neither of the great nuclear powers would wish again to move so near to the brink of war was balanced by the realization that nothing essential had yet been settled. This remained true even after the signing of the nuclear test ban treaty in August 1963, which, welcome as it was, did not in the end amount to much more than a formal recognition by the nuclear powers who signed it of their growing mutual interest in this one particular field.

The state of the Cold War at the beginning of 1964 might thus be described as one in which considerable efforts were being made to keep tensions below the level at which serious danger of nuclear war might result, while the positions of the respective sides were being stolidly maintained on all matters in dispute. These matters were, and still are, numerous and some of them are potentially dangerous. The most long-standing of them is the question of Berlin and the division of Germany. On this no progress has been made at all, and if the fear of war in Europe is less than it was, this is not because solutions are in sight but simply because, in current conditions of nuclear strategy, and in the light of the Cuba experience, the stakes are seen to be unacceptably high. It seems likely, indeed, that the nuclear stalemate, while offering a certain rather precarious assurance against all-out war, also increases the difficulty of resolving particular conflicts by negotiation. For, by ruling out the use of force as an ultimate sanction, it also removes the incentive to avoid war by the traditional method of compromise. Disputes, which would previously have been settled either by fighting or by negotiation under the threat of it, may now simply linger on unresolved, preventing any genuine improvement in international relations, yet not normally giving rise to serious fear of major war.

This is truer of those disputes where the issues are clear-cut and the stakes obviously high, as in Europe, than it is of more confused situations in areas like South East Asia or the Middle East. In some of these, the desire to ensure that local hostilities are never allowed to escalate into great-power conflict may eventually produce some form of neutrality or non-alignment, which offers hope of permanent stability, but nowhere is this process likely to be rapid and nowhere will it be easy at first to feel that the permanence is assured.

Continuing causes of friction

These reflections suggest that East-West relations over the next decade are likely to undergo only a slow and painful evolution and that to look for either quick solutions of particular problems or any dramatic transformation of the overall relationship of the principal powers would be unrealistic. The advance signs of a long-term improvement are indeed there to be seen. In the narrow but important field of nuclear weapons, and probably only in that field, a piece of common ground can already be identified. The task of Western diplomacy is to enlarge the area of common interest, principally through its defence and disarmament policies, in the meantime seeking slowly to blunt the edge of the ideological conflict, which is often the main reason for the particular disputes which arise all around the world.

Given the instability of so many areas from which imperial rule has been withdrawn and the revolutionary doctrines to which the communist powers still subscribe, it must be expected that there will be many situations in which the Western powers will continue to clash with the Soviet Union for some time to come, and perhaps even more with China. This is likely to occur not only where the decolonization process has run into trouble, as in the Congo in 1960, but equally in areas where relations between newly independent countries and former colonial powers are good, as in East Africa. In such areas urgent and explosive social problems have to be solved and tension will frequently be high. It is in the nature of things that the desire of the Western world to see these situations evolve peacefully will often be in conflict with attempts by the Soviet Union or China to exploit the possibilities of revolution which, apart from its ideological attractions, offers them the best chance of supplanting Western influence in the area. There is reason to hope that both sides will be concerned to prevent quarrels of this kind from resulting in direct conflict between the great powers, and it will be one of the most important functions of the United Nations to develop the machinery which can help to do this. But the existence of so many potential causes of dispute is likely to make the achievement of an all-round *détente* between East and West a slow business, requiring patient and far-sighted diplomacy in many anxious situations over a long period.

The elements which combine to make up East-West relations are so diverse and affect so many different areas that no one country can hope to handle them alone, not even the United States or the Soviet Union. What Britain in particular can do will depend very largely on her ability to carry others along with her. Purely national initiatives, which do not secure the co-operation of a substantial number of other powers, notably the United States and the principal states of Europe, are unlikely to make any important impact upon Soviet, let alone Chinese, policy-makers. It is not, after all, British military strength or intentions that concern Moscow, but the strength and intentions of the West as a whole, especially of the United States. Nor can British interests anywhere in the world be considered any longer as exclusively British and thus a possible subject of purely bilateral negotiation with the East. Britain's scope for effective action, like that of most other countries, is limited to what she can persuade others to join with her in doing. In the context of East-West relations this means very largely those countries to which she has been joined in alliance within NATO for the past fifteen years.

Inasmuch as the matters at issue between East and West have not been solved and are in some cases kept from erupting into violence only by fear of the consequence of modern war, it seems to follow that the West must, for the foreseeable future, maintain adequate policies of defence and deterrence. Whatever this may imply in terms of military organization and of the levels of defence budgets, the need for overall solidarity for these purposes among the Atlantic powers and particularly between the United States and her European allies, including Britain, is fairly obvious. What has often been doubted in the past, especially by those who feel that the purely military threat from the Soviet Union has been exaggerated, is whether the maintenance of a united Western bloc of nations, under United States leadership, provides an equally appropriate instrument for negotiation.

There does not seem to be much doubt what answer would now be given to this question by both the main powers concerned, the United States and the Soviet Union. Since 1960 a continuous and largely exclusive dialogue has been maintained between them. Since Cuba, their special joint responsibility in time of crisis has been recognized by the installation of the so-called 'hot line' between Washington and Moscow. Although within both the Eastern and Western alliances there are signs of the European allies asserting their right to a greater share in political and strategic decisions, when it comes to dealings between the blocs, the primacy of the two great powers has been increasingly evident. The strains which this has been producing within the Atlantic alliance will be discussed later. So far as the Soviet Union is concerned, a significant change of attitude towards Western solidarity can be detected.

For some years after the war it was a prime object of Soviet policy to keep the West divided and especially to split Western Europe from the United States. In this context the break-away proclivities of de Gaulle, based as they are specifically upon the concept of Europe's separateness from America, might have been expected to meet with Soviet support. But when de Gaulle gave his views their clearest expression, in bringing the negotiations between Britain and the Six to an end in January 1963, there was no welcome from Moscow. Whatever the precise reason for this, it seems clear that the Soviet Union would now prefer to be able to deal with the United States, especially in nuclear matters, and to have the assurance that the United States could speak for all other centres of military power in the West.

The 'bipolarization' of power

No doubt the Cuban experience brought home to Khrushchev, as to Kennedy, the need to concentrate the power of decision on both sides in time of crisis. In addition to that, the alternative prospect of separate centres of European nuclear power growing up, in which Western Germany would eventually be bound to find a place, was not likely to appeal to the Kremlin. Even de Gaulle's suggestion that, at some future time, Western Europe and the Soviet Union might more readily agree with one another once the Americans had taken themselves off to their own hemisphere, with all that that implies in terms of the emergence of a third force in Europe, received no encouragement from Khrushchev. Evidently Moscow now thinks it more important to negotiate effectively with the West as a whole, than to seek to disrupt it in order the better to deal with its disunited parts. Once again one can see the determining influence of the nuclear situation, in which the overriding consideration, for the avoidance of war, is to bring the manufacture, organization, and use of nuclear weapons under effective and, so far as may be, rational control.

There is, of course, a powerful school of thought which, so far from accepting this argument, has always opposed the so-called 'bipolarization' of power in the post-war years and welcomes any sign of a return to a greater diversification on both sides of the Iron Curtain, whether it be the split between China and Russia or the recent claims made in Western Europe to a position of parity with the United States. There is little doubt that the overwhelming pre-eminence of the United States and the Soviet Union after 1945 was a temporary phenomenon and that it is already passing, as other areas of the world recover from the effects of war and revolution. Something will be said later about the Sino-Soviet dispute. So far as the West is concerned, the recovery of the allies of the United States and the increased influence within the alliance which results from it are welcome in themselves. But so long as the East-West division continues, it is quite another thing to argue that the solidarity of the Western alliance is a disadvantage when it comes to dealing with the East.

The idea that this might be so is in part a legacy from the period, from 1950 onwards, when Western policy was for a time conducted under the slogan of 'negotiation from strength'. There was nothing wrong with this concept in itself, for no one who seeks to negotiate would prefer to do so from weakness. But the manner in which the principle was applied in practice, especially in the hands of Dulles, seemed to show that the desire to negotiate was weak, while the strength that was envisaged was the sort of strength necessary to enable one to dictate to an opponent rather than to negotiate with him on terms of reasonable equality. Since strength of this order was never attained, the policy came to have the appearance of being both disingenuous and unreal.

It may be relevant to recall the lessons of this failure

of policy at the present time, when there is still argument about the levels of military strength which the West should seek to maintain. It may be that the United States is still seeking for a margin of military superiority over her adversary, beyond what would be likely to offer the best prospect of negotiation, while still stopping far short of what would be required to enable her to dictate terms, an objective which, in modern conditions, is in any case unattainable. But however that may be (and it is not proposed to pursue the question further here), it would be hard to argue now that a splitting up of the Western alliance would be likely to promote more effective negotiation or that Western solidarity is now an obstacle to it.

So far as Britain is concerned, no major political party has, for some years, sought to argue anything of this kind, though there have from time to time been suggestions by minority groups that if Britain were to defect from the Western alliance and place herself among the non-aligned powers in world affairs, this might offer a better prospect of East-West agreement than is to be expected from the stark confrontation of two solid military blocs. If this view is not much in favour now, this is probably because of the direct dialogue between Washington and Moscow, which, as already noted, has developed since 1960. In this dialogue there seems to be no very useful, let alone influential, part to be played by any third party, who is allied to neither of the great powers. Today the role of a medium power which wishes to have a voice in the affairs of greater powers lies in working within an alliance so as to influence the policy of the whole, rather than in standing outside and playing the part of conciliator. Non-alignment, whatever its other attractions may be for some powers, no longer looks like a good technique for exerting influence in East-West relations. Recent Indian experience is generally held to bear out this view.

The Gaullist 'third force' concept

Current Gaullism, whose failure to attract Soviet support in this connexion has already been noted, embodies a 'third force' concept of a different kind. It is based upon the assumption that Europe, led by France, can be strong enough, in all spheres including the military, to deal with the Soviet Union not as a conciliator or mediator, but in its own right as a great power and in its own interests. The need to pursue such a policy is predicated upon two further assumptions: firstly that the interests of the United States and Europe are different *vis-à-vis* the East and are likely to diverge farther; and secondly that, largely for this reason, the United States will, within a decade, have lost interest in shouldering responsibility for Europe's security. On this basis, the task for Europe is to build up a European unit of power, possessing its own nuclear forces and capable of using them independently of the United States. Although, in the immediate future, Europe has to rely on the protection of the United States deterrent, no long-term solidarity between the two continents is expected or wanted.

So far as relations between East and West in Europe are concerned, it is not easy to see why American and European interests should come to diverge so sharply. During most of the post-war period this view has not been shared by German governments, whose national interests are far more intimately affected than France's. Only during the last two or three years of Adenauer's regime did there seem to be any weakening in German reliance upon the American connexion, owing to a certain suspicion which the old Chancellor had developed about the young regime in Washington and to his desire to reach agreement with France at almost any cost before his retirement. The new Erhard–Schröder team which took over in October 1963 soon reverted to the earlier German faith in Atlantic solidarity.

It is equally difficult to understand why the Soviet Union should be expected to prove more amenable over European problems if she were discussing them with Europeans alone, unbacked by American power. These propositions have never been elucidated by de Gaulle and may well be no more than a rationalization of his own deep emotional rejection of the American connexion, together with his mystical belief in the greatness of France. Since he launched these rather imprecise ideas early in 1963, he has been in no hurry to apply them in practice in dealing with the East, preferring to press on with the French strategic deterrent and with the assertion of French independence of the United States. In this policy there is no place reserved for Britain, and even if there were, no British government would be likely to accept it. Co-operation with France, as will be argued later, must remain an objective of British policy, but it cannot be achieved until some changes in current Gaullist attitudes towards the United States, Britain, and the Atlantic connexion have taken place.

So far, then, as relations with the Soviet Union are concerned, the maintenance of Atlantic solidarity, for deterrence and defence and equally for negotiation, must remain a British objective. A further long period of fluctuating tensions is to be expected, during which negotiation should be patiently pursued in the belief that, at some time, a weakening of the ideological forces will make possible agreements which are at present ruled out. In terms of conflict of economic interest or of claims to territory, the main antagonists in the Cold War have little ground for maintaining a secular hostility to one another. As the Soviet Union evolves into a conservative power, there is every reason why this fact should become steadily more apparent to her and her policies come to be based upon it.

China

The date when this might happen may be advanced by the Sino-Soviet dispute, which is already providing the Soviet Union with a motive for stabilizing her relations with the West. The rivalry between the Soviet and Chinese communist parties presents a direct ideological challenge to Soviet world influence, since both the Soviet Union and China are competing for the allegiance of the same people, especially in Asia and Africa. There are moreover substantial possibilities of dispute between the Soviet Union and China over practical questions arising along their long common frontier. There is a natural tendency to ask how this split, in what had come to be regarded as the enemy camp, should be exploited by the West. The answer, at least for the time being, is probably that not much can be done.

It is not even clear where the long-term interest of the West lies in this matter. If the split in the communist camp has the effect of reducing the pressures which have been exerted around the world by the Soviet Union since the 1917 Revolution, and especially since 1945, this will no doubt be clear gain, though Sino-Soviet rivalry for the leadership of world revolution could equally well operate to force the Soviet Union into extreme postures which she would otherwise prefer to abandon.

In any case the West would be wise not to try to base improved relations with the Soviet Union upon forming a common front against China. China is potentially a very great power, which in due course will have nuclear weapons. She can neither be destroyed nor ignored, and the long-term aim must be, as it has become with the

Soviet Union, to find a way of drawing her into international society rather than to push her farther into the wilderness. The process should start now, for, when she has already become a major military power, it may be too late. At the present time what can be done is only marginal. Communist China should be represented in the United Nations, and in this and other ways more normal relations with her should be sought. But the change which this might cause in her attitude would not be spectacular or immediate. All it could do would be to offer greater opportunities than now exist for breaking down China's isolation from so much of the world. In the meantime, Chinese aggression should be no more tolerated than any other, and her tendency to expand must be resisted when it takes the form of military attack or armed subversion. This having been said, however, it has to be recognized that stable conditions in East and South East Asia are not likely to be secured unless China is a party to the settlement. The fact that China's present mood is not favourable to such a result cannot affect the need to work for it as a long-term aim of policy.

In policy towards China, where Britain has been at loggerheads with the United States for more than a decade, the importance of carrying others with one, if one wishes to be effective, has been strikingly illustrated. Britain's separate recognition of China, announced in 1950 in the belief that many others would follow suit, has had little effect either upon Chinese action or upon events in East Asia, because British power alone was no longer sufficient for the purpose. If anything is to be effected now, it is in Washington rather than in Peking that influence will have to be exerted.

Although this is particularly true in relation to China, the same principle applies generally to the conduct of East-West relations. The point is not that there is no room for British initiatives, but that these initiatives can be effective only if they are directed first to influencing Britain's allies rather than to independent British-Soviet or British-Chinese negotiations, which do not impress the opposite party and do little more than cause irritation both among Britain's European allies and in the United States.

3

The Shape of the Western Alliance

IF it is accepted that the tensions of the Cold War are likely to be with us, perhaps in modified form, for some years to come, the maintenance of a collective organization in the West, linking the United States to Europe in a common protective effort, is a natural objective of Western policy.

The Atlantic Alliance

Obviously the existing regional defence pact, NATO, open to reconsideration in any event in 1969, has a central part in this concept, but it would be wrong to confine discussion wholly to the military sphere. For the Cold War has done more than set up a military barrier in Europe. It has divided not only Europe but much of the world into separate economic markets and areas of political influence, and affects the relations between North and South only a little less than those between East and West. What is required in the West, therefore, is the construction of a system of co-operation, which includes whatever military alliance may be necessary, but extends also to political and economic policies, especially to those which can contribute to the promotion of world trade and to the economic progress of the less developed continents.

For defence, this implies something more than a mere agreement among wholly independent powers to come to each other's aid. The need, in modern conditions, for joint command, and the pooling of logistical systems was recognized when NATO was formed and the evolution of nuclear weapons is now giving new urgency to these problems, which NATO has not been notably successful in solving in their original context. Faced with the possibility of further national nuclear forces being set up under independent national commands, NATO must now move forward to a more sophisticated system for the control of nuclear weapons or risk an eventual disintegration into separate national units.

For other purposes, such as trade and tariff policies and international aid, it is probably neither necessary nor indeed realistic to contemplate a highly institutionalized system covering all the Western countries. The concept of an Atlantic Community is valid when it is used simply to express the idea that all the countries of the area share some common purposes and should endeavour by many and varied devices to co-operate with one another to achieve them. It is misleading when it is used to suggest that it would be possible in the near future to create for the whole Atlantic area an institutionalized community of the kind which is being attempted in Europe. One does not need to be a Gaullist in order to feel that an attempt at the present time to bring Western Europe and North America under common institutions would, even if one could imagine it being acceptable in America, have the effect of swamping the real prospect of unity in Europe for the sake of a larger concept which is unreal or at least premature. As Jean Monnet wrote:[1] 'The art of political creation . . . is to obtain from countries the effective acceptance of common rules at the point where a common interest between them, however limited, emerges as a

[1] Carnegie Endowment for International Peace, *Perspectives on Peace, 1910–1960* (1960), p. 105.

necessity.' So far the Atlantic countries have moved only a short distance towards this point. The acceptance of common rules has occurred principally in the organization of joint defence, and even there it is now uncertain whether the progress made will be maintained.

In NATO's first decade the overwhelming superiority of the United States over its allies determined the structure of the alliance. It was an American enterprise, tempered only by American good sense and the need to enlist co-operation and to create a collective morale among the European allies. In recent years this pattern has been slowly changing owing to a variety of causes—the recovery of Europe, the size of the German conventional contribution, the American desire to spread the financial load, and the attitude of Gaullist France, which in turn has been closely linked to the developing problem of nuclear weapons. For all these reasons, no one now doubts that much new thinking about the nature of the NATO partnership will be required if the alliance is to obtain a new lease of effective life after 1969. Ideally the new formula should meet two requirements which appear, superficially at least, to exclude one another: the requirement that the European partners should have an effective share in the nuclear strategy on which their very existence may depend, and the requirement, clearly shown in the Cuban affair of 1962, that there should be centralized decision about the use of Western nuclear power whenever an emergency arises. The reconciliation of these two requirements is made doubly difficult by the fact that de Gaulle does not at present appear to accept the need to reconcile them and aims instead at total freedom of action for France. Whether this attitude is a purely temporary and tactical one or represents permanent French policy is one of the imponderables upon which some judgement must be attempted.

The posture which Britain has so far adopted, though understandable, has done little to help towards a solution of these questions. On the one hand she has been readier than most Continental Europeans to accept United States leadership. This is principally because of her tradition of close collaboration with the United States and the confidence derived from exchanging information with her ally on nuclear questions. Britain has in fact enjoyed an unacknowledged position of privilege in Washington, which has given her comfort as much as it has irritated other allies. On the other hand, Britain has continued to insist upon the independence of her own nuclear deterrent, thereby ensuring that France, at least, can insist on nothing less. At the same time she has contrived to imply that this French insistence is in some way anti-social while hers is not and that a similar attitude on the part of the German Federal Republic or any other state would be a positive menace.

The American Grand Design

This has been one of the reasons why many Europeans, by no means limited to Gaullists, continued to suspect, throughout the Brussels negotiations, that Britain was clinging to the special nuclear relationship with the United States, which distinguishes her from other Europeans, and was still refusing to identify herself fully with the rest of Europe within the wider Atlantic alliance. After the Kennedy administration took over in 1961, this British attitude, in addition to arousing European doubts, increasingly also cut across the American vision of the alliance's future. While Britain was discussing her possible membership of the European Economic Community in almost purely economic terms and tended to play down its political implications, the United States was coming to see it as one aspect of a political 'Grand Design' for the Western alliance as a whole and, even more widely, as part of a developing concept for the whole of the non-communist world, embracing such things as the Kennedy round of tariff reductions and world-wide policies for trade and aid.

The Grand Design was based upon the idea of an equal partnership between the United States and a steadily uniting Europe, an alliance resting upon two equal pillars. The Americans favoured United Europe because it offered the hope of a stronger bulwark against communism and a larger European contribution to the cost of European defence. That Britain should be a part of United Europe, though not perhaps indispensable, was thought important, because of the belief that Britain would bring to Europe additional political stability and a powerful reinforcement for those European elements which were seeking to make the new Europe a liberal and outward-looking community, with world trading policies which would fit well into the overall American design. The fact that British entry into the Community would spell the end of Commonwealth preference, never a popular concept in the United States, was no doubt felt to provide some compensation for the inevitable tariff discrimination by the European Economic Community against the United States.

It was significant for Britain that, if she chose to remain outside, American plans did not seem to reserve any very favourable alternative position for her. The two pillars of the alliance would still be the United States and Europe, and Britain, if she was not a part of Europe, would be likely to find herself at the margin of power and no longer at the centre. The consequence of this was that, whereas entry into Europe had formerly seemed liable to prejudice the British position in Washington, it now appeared to be a condition of preserving a satisfactory status there.

Looking back, it seems curious that the United States government, in promoting a Grand Design based upon two equal pillars, and the British government, in accepting the concept and seeking entry into the European Economic Community in pursuance of it, should apparently have hoped to be allowed to treat the question of nuclear weapons as irrelevant to these policies. At the very time when the equal partnership of the United States and Europe was being preached on the political side in Washington, McNamara, as Secretary of Defence, was making it brutally plain, notably in his speech at Ann Arbor, Michigan, in June 1962[2] that in the vital field of nuclear weapons no equality was contemplated. At the same time he made things worse by attacking France in the most categorical terms for contemplating an independent strategic nuclear deterrent, while refraining from any equally explicit condemnation of Britain's very similar conduct. The British government, for its part, anxious no doubt to avoid giving further offence to those in Britain who were already attacking its European policy as a down-grading of British sovereignty, continued blandly to assert the independence of the British nuclear deterrent and engaged in bilateral discussions with the United States on the subject, as though this could have no bearing upon the Brussels talks, which were then working up to their final crisis.

In the end it was upon these weaknesses and ambiguities in the American and British positions that de Gaulle put his finger in bringing the Brussels negotiations to an end. He made it clear in effect that he rejected Britain as a partner in Europe primarily on account of her American connexions. He interpreted the Nassau agreement of December 1962 as a further attempt by the Anglo-Saxons to assert their nuclear exclusiveness and he ridiculed the

[2] USIS Release, 18 June 1962.

idea of an equal partnership in which nuclear power was all on one side.

It is tempting now, in retrospect, to suggest that the failure to link British nuclear policy with her attempt to join EEC was always bound to prove fatal. There is evidence that some British Ministers, in the months before the Brussels breakdown, were becoming anxious that Britain should make a gesture towards Europe over nuclear weapons in order to secure success in Brussels, but it would in any case have been difficult to find a way of handling the British nuclear problem which would have been acceptable both to the United States and to de Gaulle. It might have been sufficient if it had been found possible to leave it in abeyance until the Brussels negotiations were complete instead of highlighting it at the most inconvenient moment by concluding the agreement at Nassau. However that may be, what is important now is to consider whether, with Britain for the present excluded from EEC, the Grand Design and the two-pillars concept are still alive, where Britain can now best find her place in the Western world, and what leverage she possesses for bending events to her purposes.

Possible alternatives

One way to decide whether the two-pillars concept is still alive is to ask what are the possible alternatives. For a few months in early 1963 it seemed possible that the impetus towards European unity had been broken and that no European pillar would ever come into existence. A year later this already looked unlikely. The EEC had painfully got under way again. Political unity had perhaps been postponed to a somewhat remoter future, but economic unity was again being forged and the Community was working to a single policy in world trading discussions.

Another initial anxiety, that France and Germany, where Adenauer was still in control, might be intending to assume jointly the leadership of Western Europe, basing themselves upon some form of nuclear co-operation, was also short-lived. In fact de Gaulle himself was soon seen to be treating the provisions for joint consultation contained in the Franco-German Treaty in a very cavalier fashion, while the change of regime in Germany confirmed, if there had ever been a doubt about it, that Germany would not allow herself to be separated from the United States. The Italian attitude was similar, so that the American-European partnership, like the EEC, seemed destined to survive the shocks which de Gaulle was still from time to time administering. While it was still hard to foresee how far de Gaulle would press the lone-wolf policy which he had chosen for France, it already seemed clear that he would not be able to carry the rest of the Community very far along with him. Indeed it now seemed that if France refused to co-operate with the rest of the alliance in adapting to its new tasks, she would simply throw her European partners more firmly into the arms of the United States.

Although this development was to some extent reassuring to Britain, it could not be regarded as satisfactory. While it preserved the main structure of the American-European partnership, it still left France pursuing policies which hindered the constructive evolution of the alliance, and it kept Britain outside the American-European dialogue as well. Although, in the present mood of de Gaulle there may be nothing that can be done about the first and perhaps little that can immediately change the second, neither can be permanently accepted. The aim must be, sooner or later, to restore co-operation between France and her allies and to find a place for Britain in the alliance, which will enable her to exert some influence both upon events in Europe and upon the wider policies of the West. It is not easy to see how this can be done except by a revival of the concept that Britain is essentially a part of the European pillar of the alliance.

Britain and the 'two pillars' concept

Before this theme is pursued further, one alternative view of the correct British attitude to the two-pillars concept should be considered. This is that an alliance built on two equal pillars, one on each side of the Atlantic, would encourage both European and American continentalism and would end in a split. It is far better, the argument runs,[3] for the alliance to remain unequal, with Europe too weak to contemplate shedding her dependence on America and so obviously unable to withstand Soviet pressures by herself that the United States would not be tempted to withdraw to her own hemisphere. One way to promote this objective would be for Britain to remain outside Europe, thus reducing Europe's size and power, to make a smaller military contribution to European defence, and to secure influence for herself in Washington by making her main contribution to world order in other areas, notably in the Indian Ocean.

This view amounts to a sort of inverted Gaullism. It starts, like Gaullism, from the assumption that American and European interests have a tendency to diverge. Like Gaullism, it believes that if Europe were strong enough she would pursue policies which would separate her from America. But unlike Gaullism, which welcomes this prospect and would seek to promote it, it plans to prevent the divergence by deliberately keeping Europe weak and dependent.

[3] *No Tame or Minor Role* (Bow Group pamphlet, 1963).

It is not easy to see what appeal this prospect could have either in the United States, which is seeking to share her burdens more equally with Europe, or in Europe, which could hardly fail to see in it an Anglo-Saxon plot aimed at limiting Europeans to a permanently secondary role in world affairs. Even if United States co-operation in such a plan were obtainable, which is exceedingly doubtful, the resentment of Europe at a British policy based upon such objectives would be overwhelming and justified. Britain would surely be mad to embrace the view that European weakness is a long-term British interest, or that, even if it were, Britain would be able to ensure it for long. Such a policy on Britain's part would be more likely to promote a narrow and militant Europeanism, based upon a close Franco-German partnership and directed, in part at least, against Anglo-Saxon arrogance. A Gaullist Europe of a particularly dangerous kind would be the probable result.

A much more promising attitude for Britain to adopt would be that the European desire for a better status, even if it cannot in all respects amount to equality with the United States, is a legitimate one and that Britain should not try to thwart it, as she would no doubt have sought to do in previous centuries, but should help by participating in it within an overall Atlantic framework of alliance. To pursue any other policy would be to assume either that Britain, simply by keeping aloof from Europe, can ensure that Europe is too weak to pursue independent policies, or that there is no need for Britain to aim at influencing events in Europe provided that, by her role in other parts of the world, she retains a footing in Washington. Neither of these views seems tenable and the argument therefore turns back to the way in which Britain may best secure for herself an effective place in an alliance, which still seems likely to be based upon a strong American pillar and a

European pillar which, if not as strong as the American, will be much stronger in the future than it has been in the past and will in any event be stronger than Britain can be by herself.

It has already been conceded that there is nothing Britain can do to secure immediate entry into the Community so as to become effectively a part of the European pillar. All she can do is to work towards this end by pursuing policies which are consistent with this eventual result and, if possible, give to France's partners in the Six an incentive to assist this process, and to give to France in due course an incentive to change her attitude.

What this implies for British economic policy, whether in the Commonwealth, EFTA or the GATT, will be considered in due course. The question which now concerns us is whether Britain can any longer expect to be considered a suitable partner by Europeans unless she is willing to accept equal status with her European colleagues in nuclear as well as conventional forces. This does not necessarily mean Britain giving up her nuclear capability. France, after all, is in the Community, and although, under de Gaulle, she is proving a most awkward partner, it is not primarily her strategic deterrent that is causing the trouble. Thus Britain's manufacture and possession of nuclear weapons is not of itself an insuperable obstacle to integration with Europe. What may prove to be an insuperable obstacle is the prolongation into the next phase of allied policy of the special privileges which Britain has enjoyed in Washington in the field of nuclear weapons. These have not so far been available to any other European power and have thus tended to emphasize Britain's essential separateness from her European neighbours.

The Nassau agreement

In this context, the Anglo-American agreement signed at Nassau in the Bahamas in December 1962, though highly favourable to Britain from one point of view, nevertheless appears as a dubious stroke of policy. While one part of it purported to offer to France, for the first time, American co-operation in the production of a strategic deterrent force on the same terms as were being offered to Britain, de Gaulle had no difficulty in showing, in his famous press conference in January 1963, that the proposition was not well designed to meet French needs. It had in fact been worked out between Americans and British to correspond with British requirements, and the invitation to France to join in an agreement which she had not helped to negotiate only served to exacerbate relations between the Anglo-Saxons and the French President at a particularly unfortunate moment.

Another odd feature of the Nassau agreement was that it was capable of being presented to the British public as a guarantee of the independence of the British nuclear deterrent for an indefinite time ahead, while Europeans, as well as the official British Opposition, took it as a sign that, whatever words might be employed, Britain's nuclear power was in future to be dependent upon the United States.

In retrospect what the Nassau agreement can be seen to have achieved for Britain was the possibility of obtaining, largely at American expense, a strategic weapon which, once delivered to her, would be under her national command and could therefore, in theory at least, be used in a crisis independently of United States policy. Despite the assurances that American technical help would be given on a continuing basis, it remains uncertain for how long this agreement will really enable Britain to retain a strategic nuclear capability with even this limited degree of independence. When the time comes to face the next phase of weapons development, the likelihood of Britain again being able to secure such generous terms from the United States seems small and the likelihood of her then deciding to resume full independence in the production of her own weapons is nil.

That de Gaulle, in the present phase of his thinking about France's renewed national grandeur, might have accepted anything similar for himself was never conceivable. Before it could become conceivable, he would have to change his mind about France's capacity to create and maintain by her own unaided effort an effective strategic deterrent. Such a change of mind is not to be ruled out, for France is, in fact, worse placed than Britain to keep in the nuclear race unaided. If she were to continue on her present course, she would be likely in the long run to overstrain her economy in a futile effort to produce weapons, which would always be obsolete before they were available for use. Nothing in the French political or economic position suggests that France's nuclear effort will be so stepped up as to avoid this result. The only other expedient, the uniting of French and German industrial capacity for this purpose, would involve an evolution in the German position which is not at present in sight and, if the problems of the alliance are wisely handled in the next few years, should never take place.

For these reasons, which must be as apparent in Paris as they are elsewhere, it is not unreasonable for France's allies to calculate that the present French intransigence may well be temporary and that France's co-operation might eventually be secured if well-considered policies were followed by the rest of the alliance. The object of such policies would be to organize a degree of inter-allied co-operation in formulating nuclear strategic doctrine and

The Shape of the Western Alliance

in the planning of its execution, which would enable the allies of the United States to accept with confidence the need for the United States President to have the last word in the operational control of Western nuclear action. Britain already very largely has this confidence and consequently accepts this need. This is because she has actually been participating, even if somewhat marginally, in nuclear strategy and is consequently informed about what it involves and because she has a well-established habit of co-operation with the United States in these matters.

The countries of continental Europe have not had these advantages and France is now leading a revolt against the continuance of the situation. Characteristically de Gaulle is pressing his claims in a manner and to an extreme, which most Europeans find excessive, but many of them feel that the time has come when they are at least entitled to be treated by the United States as Britain has been treated in the past. In order to achieve this, most of them, and the Germans in particular, hope that it may not be necessary for them to contemplate anything comparable with the British independent nuclear force, which has been the basis of the special British position in the past, for the dangers and complications of this are clear enough. But a genuine share in the making of the strategic policies of the West they feel to be their due. If every other way of obtaining it were closed to them, they might eventually seek it by joining with France in her current posture of somewhat hostile self-assertion against the United States. While this need not necessarily be disastrous, it scarcely needs arguing that a development of this kind would almost preclude rational co-operation within the Western alliance, while it would also be likely to raise tension between Western Europe and the Soviet bloc.

Britain, on the face of it, should have some leverage here in influencing European attitudes. Indeed this may be the only effective leverage she possesses in Europe at the present time. She has not used it yet, because of her dual insistence upon the independence of her deterrent and upon her special American link. For this she has advanced two reasons.

The first is that unless her independence is visibly preserved, a potential opponent might attack Britain in the mistaken belief that the United States would fail to support her out of fear of Soviet retaliation on American cities.[4] That the British government did not itself believe that a Soviet threat to Britain could be deterred by anything less than a combination of United States and British nuclear power was stated in terms by Lord Home in 1963 when he was Foreign Secretary.[5] Whether independent British action would seem more credible to the Soviet High Command than it seemed to him is at least doubtful.

The second reason given is that the independent deterrent buys for Britain enhanced status in Washington and in negotiations among the great powers. It may be conceded that it has done so in the past, but it seems less likely to do so in future, as the independent British capability dwindles. In any case the argument is operative only in reply to a proposal that Britain should drop out of the nuclear arms business altogether. It does not have much weight against a proposal for making a British contribution to a nuclear force under collective control. If a satisfactory system of this kind could be devised, it would serve the double purpose of permitting Britain to retain whatever status a nuclear capability may be thought to confer

---

[4] This argument is set out in the official Statement on Defence, 1964 (Cmnd. 2270).

[5] Lord Home, speaking at the Canadian Club, Ottawa, on 21 May 1963, was reported in *The Times* of 22 May to have said that thousands of Soviet nuclear missiles 'are trained on our island'. This 'colossal threat' could be deterred only by the combination of United States and British nuclear power.

The Shape of the Western Alliance

and at the same time of contributing to the solidarity of the Western alliance. To achieve this would require some sacrifice by Britain of her independence, which already seems more theoretical than real, and a willingness on the part of the United States to share some of her responsibilities more widely. For the reasons already mentioned, this is probably the price which the United States will in any case have to pay for continuing leadership of an effective coalition in the coming decade.

The Mixed-Manned Force

That the United States has been ahead of Britain in feeling her way towards a solution of this kind is suggested by her promotion in 1963 of the Multilateral or Mixed-Manned Force (MLF) of nuclear-armed vessels. Few people imagine that this proposal represents a very efficient way of enabling Europeans to contribute to the military strength of the alliance; nor does it, in its initial form, guarantee to the allies of the United States an effective voice in the management of the main Western deterrent forces. By itself the MLF is therefore probably too marginal to military requirements to have a major political effect. Nevertheless, taken in conjunction with other developments, such as the setting up of a NATO Nuclear Committee, the special international nuclear staff at SHAPE, and the presence of allied officers at the Headquarters of the American Strategic Air Command in Omaha, it is possible to see the MLF as the beginning of a system within NATO which might reconcile the twin objectives of widely spread consultation and effectively centralized command.

The particular contribution which the MLF makes to this process is the concept of actual participation by nationals of the various countries, without the governments concerned acquiring thereby the power of independent action. Some such element of practical participation by the allies of the United States seems essential as a basis for genuine consultation, for without it any machinery which might be created for consultation between a major ally who is bearing all the responsibility and a group of minor allies who are bearing none is likely to be a mere façade. The disparity between the American and the European contributions to the Western nuclear effort is bound in any event to be very wide, but the readiness of the United States to give information and the capacity of her allies to understand and assess it would be much enhanced by even a limited practical European participation in the day-to-day working of a nuclear force. The MLF also introduces the concept that some European financial contribution should be made, and this has the advantage of carrying with it an enhanced sense of responsibility for the efficiency of the enterprise and, on the American side, provides an incentive to build the force eventually into a genuine instrument of joint defence, to which Europeans might eventually think it worth while to contribute substantially.

Collective nuclear defence

It is important to be clear about the reason why major reorganization of the nuclear resources of the Western alliance is necessary. It is not because of a need to increase the overall nuclear strength of the alliance *vis-à-vis* the Soviet Union, for the United States is already more than strong enough. Nor is it primarily because of the desire of the United States to get her allies to accept a larger part of the burden, for she could probably lighten her own burden at least as much by unilateral action.

The reason is rather that the present nuclear preoccupations of Western countries are showing an unmistakable tendency to fragment the alliance, whose continuation for both political and military purposes is still desirable. European confidence in the protection afforded by the American deterrent has weakened just at the moment when European recovery is in any case giving rise to legitimate demands for a larger voice in Western policy. There is thus a fairly clear choice facing the alliance between improved co-operation on the one hand or increasing separatism on the other.

De Gaulle is not the cause of this, but his anti-American bias and the high priority he gives to finding a distinct role for France have sharpened the issue and charged it with political emotions which make it harder to handle. Not only has de Gaulle called in question the continuance of American and European partnership but he has also forced the intrinsically difficult German problem once more into the forefront of allied politics.

Post-war German governments have based their hopes of equality of status with their Western colleagues upon the building of a system of collective defence in which all would surrender some sovereignty. In return for the protection offered by the Atlantic alliance they have undertaken to refrain from developing purely national nuclear capabilities. If now, under Gaullist pressures, there is to be no collective Atlantic defence, but only a number of loosely co-ordinated national defence systems, with the United States held at arm's length from Europe, future German governments will find it hard to accept indefinitely a nuclear status inferior to that of other major countries of Europe. If national separatism in nuclear weapons is allowed to grow, it will put in jeopardy not only Atlantic solidarity but also the Paris agreements of 1954, whereby the German Federal Republic undertook not to manufacture atomic weapons.

In this situation something needs to be done to meet legitimate German anxieties. German opinion is still far from demanding revision of the Paris agreements and would certainly be willing to accept an alternative which gave Germany a more effective voice in allied nuclear policy without also giving her independence of action, an attitude which is reflected in the German readiness to participate in a multilateral force. If, with this as a starting point, an improved system of Western nuclear co-operation is to be evolved, both the United States and Britain will have to accept some restriction of their existing freedom of action. This is a serious problem for the United States, which enjoys vast technical superiority over her allies and shoulders unique responsibilities. For Britain, the prospective sacrifice involved in accepting a measure of allied control over her nuclear forces is much less, because her present independence is more limited and its continuation for more than a few years is uncertain. The nuclear superiority which she still enjoys in Europe makes this a favourable moment for action on her part. Later the leverage which this gives her may well be less.

Britain's action after Nassau in committing her nuclear bomber force to NATO command, albeit with a reservation in case of a threat to supreme national interests, was a step in the right direction. There is indeed at present no other authority to which it could be committed and the day when there will be an Atlantic or even a European political authority capable of taking control of a British nuclear force seems far off. In the formal sense, therefore, an element of national control in the last resort over a British nuclear force committed to allied command is bound in any case to remain for some time. In practice, the longer the force is successfully operated and trained under allied command, the less likely it is that it will ever revert to purely national control.

The Shape of the Western Alliance 49

British efforts should now be directed to developing the most effective system possible within NATO for joint planning of the use of nuclear forces among all the NATO allies. In so far as this may require the United States to extend to other NATO allies technical information which she has so far only given to Britain, Britain should encourage her to do this, and particularly to make it clear to France that this information can be made available to her if she will join Britain in operating her nuclear forces within the proposed new NATO framework. This would pave the way for a return to co-operation between France and the United States and also, by putting France on the same footing as Britain, between France and Britain. Though French acceptance of such an offer could not be expected quickly, the fact of its being known to have been made would have its effect upon the evolution of French opinion.

In the meantime the crucial problem of German participation would have to be met by improved staff collaboration within NATO over nuclear policy, including the management of the British forces committed to NATO, together with some evolution of the mixed-manned force, in which Germans would be full participants from the start. Various kinds of evolution are conceivable. If, for instance, the initial experiment in mixed-manning is successful, there will be a case for enlarging the mixed-manned force by making a growing portion of British nuclear forces a part of it. This would increase the proportion of the total Western deterrent in which European allies took part, so broadening the area of joint responsibility. This policy could be initiated without France but, if successful, would provide an incentive to France to participate eventually, an objective which has always to be kept in mind.

Any attempt to foresee the ultimate pattern of nuclear

co-operation to which these steps might lead would at present be purely speculative. It would depend, for instance, upon the progress made towards political unity in Europe and, even more, upon the extent to which future United States administrations were willing to accept some restriction of American freedom of action in nuclear strategy. It would not, in any early future, make the European pillar of the alliance the equal of the American, but, short of that, it would enable European governments to take a much larger part in the formulation of joint policies than they have done so far and would to that extent halt the process of disintegration of allied unity which has been apparent since the beginning of 1963.

An early start to this process would serve a valuable immediate purpose of a different kind for Britain. The danger of the European Economic Community beginning seriously to concert its foreign and defence policies without Britain having an opportunity to take part in the discussions or to influence European thinking has been a continuous British preoccupation, and early in 1964 formal representations were made in Europe on the subject. Britain's friends in the Community were able to ensure that, pending the 1964 elections in Britain, all doors were kept open for her, but once a new Parliament has been elected, Britain will be expected to clarify her attitude to Europe. Defence policy, and especially nuclear policy, may be the one field where she can do this at once, without risking a rebuff such as she might face if she were, for instance, to renew her application to sign the Treaty of Rome without first covering herself against a French veto.

For these various reasons, it seems likely that Britain would be well advised to use the special position which she still occupies among the nuclear powers to influence European and allied nuclear policy rather than to maintain an independent strategic deterrent indefinitely or to announce the intention to give it up. Neither of these courses would increase British influence within the alliance. Britain's allies do not feel that they obtain much benefit from an independent British deterrent, which they see as a purely national instrument; nor would they attribute any moral virtue to Britain is she abandoned her deterrent, since they would see it simply as a step forced upon her by economic and technological considerations. On the other hand a British policy which both accepted by implication Britain's equal status with her European allies and helped to halt the present trend towards the disintegration of NATO into separate national nuclear units would increase Britain's weight in Europe and within the alliance as a whole.

Opinion on the wisest way of handling the problem of nuclear armaments tends to divide along the line which separates two broad schools of thought. On the one side are those who, recognizing the many technological factors which now make for international interdependence, are anxious to develop international political institutions as fast as possible to meet the new requirements. On the other are those who, without denying the technological trend, dislike its political implications and fight tenaciously to retain the sovereign nation-state as the centre of authority for as long and in as many fields as possible. The development of nuclear weapons comes as a lifesaver to this second school of thought, by making it possible to suggest that moderate-sized nations may now be able after all to look the great powers in the eye, if they make national nuclear deterrent forces the basis of continuing national independence.

This doctrine, clearly stated by de Gaulle, appeals to deep-seated emotions in many countries including Britain and is consequently capable of stimulating dangerously nationalist ambitions at a time when every economic and military consideration underlines the need for greater international co-operation. The question which way the pendulum is going to swing may well be decided within the next few years, which are likely to see either increasing proliferation of separate national forces or the development of a growing measure of collective control. Collective control is what is required for purposes of multilateral disarmament and arms control, and it is difficult to see how this is ever to be achieved among mutually suspicious great powers if it has already been written off as impossible among allied countries who share a far higher degree of common interest.

The creation of new institutions to meet new needs is surrounded with difficulty and uncertainty, but not with greater danger than reversion to its nationalist alternative. There is a chance now for the Western powers to do some vitally important pioneering and for Britain to play a major part in the work. It is with this opportunity in mind that British nuclear policies must now be directed.

4

World Security after the End of Empire

THE last two decades have witnessed the withdrawal of the imperial powers from their widely spread dominions. The measure of the withdrawal is that the number of independent states in the world has more than doubled in this period. The former sovereign power has been removed from vast areas, often to be replaced by local inter-state rivalries, sometimes stimulated by the efforts of outside powers to spread their influence into regions where, for the time being, everything has seemed fluid.

In almost every place outside Europe where serious international complications have arisen since 1945, the trouble can be traced to the winding up of Empire and its immediate aftermath. When it is recalled that this world-shaking process has been carried on against the background of the Cold War, the wonder is not that there has been so much bloodshed but that there has been so little. In most cases, up to the moment of independence, the imperial power has insisted on its exclusive right and responsibility to maintain order, but once that moment has passed, the peace and security of the area have become a fully international concern. In the coming decade there will be few colonial areas left, and even those few are unlikely to escape international attention, as the problems of the Portuguese and the remaining British dependencies in Southern Africa already bear witness.

Normally when empire ends, the explicit commitments of the imperial power end too, as they did with the independence of India, Indo-China, Indonesia, and the Congo. But some remain, whether under treaty or for other reasons, and Britain, having possessed the largest and most varied of the empires, still has the largest and most varied responsibilities left on her hands. Her overseas commitments, outside the NATO area, present the following general picture.[1]

British overseas commitments

She is a member of two regional alliances in addition to NATO, CENTO for the Middle East and SEATO for South East Asia. She also has commitments in respect of defence and of the maintenance of law and order in a diminishing number of dependencies or protectorates around the world, for which she has a direct responsibility. She has further some defence treaties with particular territories, such as Kuwait and Malaysia. She also accepts a moral, if not a legal commitment for the defence of independent members of the Commonwealth, even where there are no treaty obligations. Finally, she is a member of the United Nations.

Most of these commitments are no longer exclusively British, being shared in varying degrees with others by virtue of alliances or of joint obligations under the United Nations Charter. But some are exclusive, such as those relating to law and order in dependencies; while others are in practice primarily if not exclusively British, in the sense that Britain would be expected to be the first to respond to a call for help and consequently deploys her forces in such a way as to enable her to do so, for instance by main-

[1] The Statements on Defence for 1962–3–4 (Cmnds. 1639, 1936, and 2270).

World Security after the End of Empire 55

taining forces in Aden for possible use in aid of the Persian Gulf sheikhdoms.

In addition to these obligations in respect of land areas, the navy accepts as one of its primary roles the safeguarding of the peaceful movement of merchant shipping. In most areas this is not an exclusive role, but 'in the entire sea area east of Suez across the Indian Ocean, the Royal Navy plays the leading role in safeguarding the trade and commerce of the free world.'[2]

Finally, the navy is preparing to become the operator of a Polaris submarine fleet 'as Britain's independent contribution to the long-range deterrent forces of the Western alliance'.[3] So long as this force remains independent it is presumably held to be theoretically available to serve British ends outside the NATO area.

To fulfil her widely scattered obligations, Britain maintains overseas bases, now limited to Cyprus, Aden, and Singapore, together with a variety of garrisons and posts which provide staging and other facilities for her forces, such as Gibraltar, Malta, Libya, Gan, and Hong Kong. She also maintains a strategic mobile reserve in the United Kingdom for use in any part of the world.

In recent years the forces disposed in this manner have been concerned in a number of relatively small operations, in Jordan (1957), Muscat and Oman (1957), Kuwait (1961), British Guiana (1962 and 1964), and Brunei (1962). With the exception of the Jordan operation (which was co-ordinated with United States action in the Lebanon), all these involved action by exclusively British forces. In addition Britain reacted immediately with military aid when India was attacked by China, direct military intervention not being requested. By the end of 1963 Britain was also engaged in defence operations on a substantial scale in aid of Malaysia, in a law and order

[2] Cmnd. 1936, p. 15.   [3] Ibid.

operation in Cyprus, and early in 1964 she responded to calls for assistance in maintaining order in the newly independent countries of Kenya, Tanganyika, and Uganda.

No other power has so varied a collection of obligations. The United States is, of course, equipped to take military action all over the world but in most cases accepts commitments only for the containment of communism and maintains relatively few overseas bases. France still has substantial military commitments in Africa. The other principal non-communist industrial powers such as Germany, Italy, Japan, or Canada and Australia, have no comparable commitments at all. Only Britain still has a substantial number of scattered dependencies to guard and only Britain still has so many old treaty obligations, requiring her to intervene in purely local disputes between neighbours, especially in the Middle East.

Few of Britain's present military dispositions throughout the world were originally planned in order to meet the commitments which are now their principal justification. They represent rather what happens to be left of a system planned for different purposes, which have now passed into history. The British presence in Cyprus, for instance, was a by-product of the Eastern question in the nineteenth century; the treaties in the Persian Gulf were designed to stop piracy; while the string of bases whose purpose was once to secure the 'all-red route' to India have survived the ending of British rule at its terminal point and even the breaking in 1956 of the central link in the chain, Suez.

It does not, of course, follow that an old base may not serve a new purpose equally well, or may not at least be better than any other instrument available, but it is, on the face of it, unlikely that such a coincidence will apply throughout the whole system. There is therefore everything to be said for looking with a critical eye at these commitments, which not only dictate a large part of the British defence budget but also colour the British people's view of their own role in the world.

It is true that in the past decade the old system has served certain residual British purposes, as the imperial commitment slowly dwindled, and examples can be given, right up to 1964, when old base facilities were useful, for instance at Aden for intervention in the Persian Gulf and in East Africa. But a closer look suggests that this was essentially a transitional phenomenon, closely related to the attainment of independence and unlikely to be repeated as the date of the various transfers of power recedes into the past. Even where the possible need for future British intervention cannot be ruled out, the case for continuing to accept exclusive British responsibility is a doubtful one and its relationship to contemporary British interests needs to be closely examined. Disengagement from long-standing positions cannot, of course, be accomplished overnight, still less can treaties be repudiated without notice. But if, as seems likely, much of the old system is going to crumble in any event, it is fairer both to Britain and to those who still rely upon her to foresee and if possible to plan the transition to a newer way of doing things.

The Middle East and Far East

So far as the defence of the remaining British dependencies is concerned, in most cases, as in the Pacific and South Atlantic islands, the burden is not great enough to raise major issues of policy. There are a few exceptional cases. British troops will probably be needed for internal security in Hong Kong until such time as the colony's future is diplomatically determined. No local military measures can have much relevance to its external defence. Troops may for a time have to keep the peace in British Guiana, but this too is essentially a political problem in which the end of colonial rule surely cannot be much longer delayed. By far Britain's most serious remaining colonial problem is that of Southern Rhodesia. A solution of this by force of British arms is scarcely credible; while if military intervention anywhere in Southern Africa were to become necessary, say for the protection of the High Commission Territories or on account of some trouble in Portuguese Africa, no one can doubt that this would, from the start, be a fully international matter, in which Britain might have special but certainly no longer exclusive responsibility.

Next come commitments arising out of the Cold War, beginning with the CENTO and SEATO treaties. It has been difficult to take CENTO seriously ever since it lost all Arab support. It is claimed that, under the wing of CENTO, a certain amount of economic co-operation has been achieved and that, secretly, the organization has some counter-subversion measures to its credit, but it has no united command and its role appears to be at best marginal for all purposes. Britain, after all, needs no special treaty to facilitate routine co-operation with Turkey, a NATO colleague, or with Pakistan, a Commonwealth member. That leaves only Iran, whose exposed situation *vis-à-vis* the Soviet Union would presumably suffice, without any regional treaty, to assure her of such help and advice as the West may be willing to give her.

There is, perhaps, no need to do anything about this relatively innocuous body. The only danger lies in attaching undue importance to it, for instance by allowing the already baffling problem of Cyprus to be complicated by the assertion that the sovereign bases there are essential to provide air support for CENTO. If, as is possible, a

British element of an international force has to remain in Cyprus, it will not be for this reason, which should not be allowed to count.

SEATO's initial importance in 1954 was that it enabled the United States to throw its protection over some of the states in the area. On the ground, it scarcely exists as an effective military alliance and, in the present context, all that need be said is that the considerable British commitments in the area, including the Singapore base, are not really due to SEATO at all, but rather to Britain's treaty obligations to Malaysia and her concern for the general stability of South East Asia.

Aden[4]

These two treaties, CENTO and SEATO, might be described as a relic of the 'early Dulles period' of Western policy. They are of minor significance to Britain today. It is much more important to consider the other reasons which, it is claimed, still necessitate the British military presence in the Indian Ocean, based upon Aden at one end and Singapore at the other, with Gan as an air staging post between them.

When Britain's overseas commitments are talked of, it is essentially this area, the area formerly dominated by Britain's Indian Empire, that is meant. It is the maintenance of British forces permanently east of Suez that imposes the burden and sustains Britain's view of herself as a power different in kind from any other.

Aden's role as part of an all-red sea route effectively ended in 1956. It still has a role in the air link to Gan and Singapore. Its role in support of British oil interests in the Persian Gulf has recently dwindled, since Kuwait became independent and began to make the many overdue adjust-

---

[4] For fuller discussion of the position of Aden see Gillian King, *Imperial Outpost—Aden* (1964). (Chatham House Essays.)

ments in her relations with her neighbours. It is in everyone's interest that the other and far less important oil-bearing sheikhdoms should be encouraged to do likewise. The need for military force to protect oil supplies in future is in any case highly disputable, since there is a world oil surplus and the producers need no military inducement to sell to industrial countries. It seems most unlikely that, if the British forces based on Aden were no longer there, Britain would lose the oil supplies which she now draws from the area, but it is sometimes said that the presence of British military forces enables her to get the oil more cheaply than she might otherwise do and that, in the absence of such forces, some of what is now sterling oil would have had to be paid for in dollars.

Whatever may have been the force of such arguments in the past, when Britain's arrangements with the oil-bearing countries and sheikhdoms had to be seen in the context of her dominating position throughout the whole Middle East, they are not very convincing today, when that position has gone, and when the oil interests themselves have become so largely international in character. Europe and the United States, as well as other countries, now share with Britain the concern for a steady export of reasonably priced oil from the Persian Gulf and, in so far as this is dependent upon the political stability of the area, it will in future have to be achieved by more sophisticated methods than the local application of force by a single Western nation. Today the effectiveness of the old methods is open to doubt, while the political disadvantages which now attend the old kind of unilateral military action are not open to doubt at all.

If the 'all-red route' was the reason for the British presence in Aden in an earlier phase and was later superseded by the need to protect oil interests, it now seems necessary to recognize that a third phase is opening, in which a fresh assessment of British interests in the Aden area is again required. British achievement in settling the disturbances in various newly independent East African territories early in 1964 was taken by some as evidence that a British 'fire-brigade' force based on Aden must be maintained, since there is now no British-controlled territory in this part of Africa. But it seems unwise to assume that, in future, Britain will often be called upon to play this kind of role. As has already been pointed out, this type of incident is most likely to occur in the immediate aftermath of independence. At a later stage it is both less likely that Britain would be invited to intervene, and much less certain that she ought to be prepared to do so. It is one thing for her to accept a brief continuing responsibility for seeing that a newly-independent government has a chance to get on its feet, free from the sort of military subversion which so swiftly overtook the Congo; it is quite another thing to maintain bases permanently overseas in the expectation of being called in to prop up governments which are experiencing internal difficulties at a later stage of their independent history. In very many cases intervention of this kind would be positively wrong, especially unilateral intervention, and Britain certainly should not claim any special role for herself in this respect. To do so would be damaging to her internationally and would correspond to no modern national interest.

There remains the need for a base in Aden not for operations in its own immediate vicinity but as a link in an Indian Ocean communications system. That it has some usefulness as an air link between Britain and more distant parts of Asia is undoubtedly true, and will presumably continue to be true, so long as Singapore remains an important centre of British military activity. But this function by itself could scarcely justify the heavy cost, both in financial and in political terms, of the Aden base. South East Asia and Australasia can, after all be reached by a west-about route if necessary. In order to justify the indefinite maintenance of a permanent major base at Aden it is not enough to invoke its usefulness as a staging point on the way to somewhere else. It is also necessary to believe that Aden is essential to a more ambitious Indian Ocean strategy which Britain still has to maintain.

This strategy is often described as the filling of 'the Indian Ocean gap', a concept which gained currency in the period when the West, especially the United States, was engaged in building up a chain of alliances for the containment of communism. Europe and the Atlantic, the Middle East and South East Asia all had their appropriate defensive organizations, at least on paper. In the Far East, the United States was well equipped with bases. Only between Aden and Singapore was there a military vacuum.

The filling of the 'Indian Ocean gap' is seen by many strategists as a necessity and as something which is Britain's peculiar obligation. But this should be challenged. Britain's presence in this area in earlier generations was due to her need to protect both trade and possessions from other European maritime powers, as well as to supply her own forces in India, which were the main safeguard for her Indian Empire against any encroachment overland from the north. Today the threat from maritime powers external to the area is virtually non-existent. The threat overland from the north, if it were to require international intervention of any kind, would certainly not be much affected by a British presence in Aden, or indeed in Singapore. It could only be countered either by invoking the nuclear deterrent, which is already global in character, or by the application of massive international military force, operating by invitation from the Indian sub-continent. In neither case could there be any question of Britain being more than one important element in a wider international enterprise, carried out on a scale which would make the existing British establishments in the Indian Ocean seem wholly marginal.

In fact this type of major military threat to the area is fanciful, at least so far as the Soviet Union is concerned, and whatever calculations may be made about possible Chinese military ambitions, the means for countering them are surely not to be found in Britain's traditional Indian Ocean bases. The infiltration of Soviet or Chinese influence by means other than military attack is a more likely development, and the retention of British strongpoints, especially Aden, is more likely to offer opportunities to Soviet and Chinese diplomacy than to present effective obstacles to them.

It is therefore not clear that the filling of the so-called 'Indian Ocean gap' represents anything real in terms of strategy, unless, like the White Knight, one is determined to be permanently equipped everywhere for even the most unlikely contingencies. There is necessarily a streak of the White Knight in the thinking of military planners, who are required by their governments and inclined by their training to prepare for the worst and to think primarily of a prospective enemy's capability before assessing his probable intentions. Britain, in her approach to world security, is perhaps addicted more than most to this type of thinking, for she has been accustomed for generations to the idea that she should have permanent footholds at reasonable intervals all over the world from which to promote her endlessly varied interests. Consequently, any gap arouses apprehensions, even where it is not obviously related to any identifiable threat.

If one starts with this general approach, it is easy to convince oneself that the Aden base is still indispensable, and one is then drawn inexorably to accept the costly and frustrating process of intervention in the affairs of the Arabian peninsula, in which Britain has now been unrewardingly engaged for a number of years, without even earning the whole-hearted support of other Western countries, whose joint interests her efforts are supposed to serve. If joint Western interests really are involved, more should be done to persuade other countries to accept some share of the burden of defending them, but the attempt is not likely to succeed unless better arguments can be found than have so far been adduced. In the meantime, the conclusion must be that military expenditure on the Aden base is disproportionate to any British interest which is now at stake, while the political backwash of Britain's consequent involvement in South Arabian politics does her gratuitous damage both in the Middle East and farther afield.

Singapore

The British commitment in Singapore is more relevant to modern conditions than the Aden base and for that reason may be more durable. Britain has retained her position in Singapore, after the independence of Malaya and the establishment of Malaysia, in return for the undertaking in her bilateral defence treaty to defend the newly independent state. So long as she is required for this purpose, she will presumably be invited and will consent to stay.

The immediate cause of her involvement in military operations at the end of 1963 was, of course, the refusal of Indonesia to recognize the new state and her policy of 'confrontation' in North Borneo. Though Indonesian hostility was no surprise, the recklessness shown was something that could hardly have been foreseen, nor can anyone be certain how permanent it will be. The formation of the state of Malaysia was a condition without which it would not have been possible for Britain to complete the decolonization of the area. If she had baulked at the final stages of this process on whatever pretext, the violence of the Indonesian reaction would no doubt have been greater still, so that there is no need for self-reproach over the action which has put Britain in her present uncomfortable position.

That it is particularly uncomfortable is due to the fact that the United States, Australia, and New Zealand are all deeply concerned to avoid involvement in hostilities with Indonesia, whom they are anxious eventually to build up into a bulwark against Chinese or communist domination of the area. Not sharing Britain's direct responsibility under her defence treaty to protect Malaysia against all comers, they direct their efforts primarily to securing some political settlement with Indonesia, while in the meantime Britain incurs the main odium of preventing a solution by force of arms.

In view of rumblings of dissension between Britain and the United States over this question early in 1964, and of a feeling sometimes expressed in Britain that it is time for her Commonwealth colleagues to give her better support, it is important for Britain to take a long view about the role she has to play in this area. In the short run she is admittedly shouldering the burden of defending Malaysia alone, and the price which she may have to pay for this in the end includes the transfer to others, in no very distant future, of the predominant position which she has enjoyed in South East Asian affairs for more than a century. She may in the end be, as it were, the scapegoat, whose expulsion makes it possible for others to negotiate a more peaceful and more lasting settlement than could be realized so long as even the appearance remained of Britain's former imperial position.

If this is correct, then those for whom Indonesian co-operation is an overriding long-term objective may be right to leave most of the dirty work to Britain and even, later on, to support a solution which appears to do Britain an injustice by requiring the elimination, or at least the curtailment, of British power in this part of the world. Hard as it may be for Britain to accept this, she might be wise to adopt it as the objective of her own policy and to regard the price as worth paying. For Britain's long-term interest does not lie in the indefinite maintenance of British forces in South East Asia for the protection of British commercial interests, but rather in securing a political settlement within the area which makes the presence of Western armed forces, including her own, unnecessary as a shield against attack from within the area.

So far as the external defence of the area is concerned, it is not Britain but the United States which has been its principal guarantor ever since the fall of Singapore in 1942, and in the long run her surest allies for the purpose will be Australia and New Zealand. It is important for their future as guarantors against external aggression that they should not, in this early stage of post-imperial politics, incur the lasting hostility of Indonesia, whose allies in external defence they may shortly wish to become. In the long run this is also the interest of Malaysia itself, though her room for manoeuvre is obviously limited so long as she is subject to direct Indonesian attack.

It is obvious that a development of this kind, which is by no means fanciful, would put considerable strain upon Britain's relations with her allies and might prove intolerable, unless Britain had in the meantime succeeded in reformulating the objectives of her military strategy overseas and had obtained political acceptance of them among her own people. This would require the recognition that her present role in Singapore is a transitional one and

World Security after the End of Empire 67

that, so far from seeking to maintain it for years ahead, she actually wishes to liquidate it once the threat to Malaysia has abated; that she is prepared to take the burden of holding the line until a long-term settlement is in sight; but that, once that moment comes, the widest sharing of the responsibility for peace and security rather than the preservation of a special British position is her aim.

The setting of an objective of this kind would not, of course, immediately relieve Britain of any existing burden. Indeed it might lead her to accept the sole burden of operations in defence of Malaysia for an appreciable period, in the belief that, by relieving her allies of the necessity of joining in, she would be facilitating their efforts to find a settlement.

What is being proposed is therefore in no sense a 'little England' policy of abdicating responsibility. It is the conscious acceptance of transitional responsibility, however unrewarding, with the declared objective of completing, in the sphere of military security, the liquidation of Empire and its transformation into more modern forms of collective security.

An international security system

Two main difficulties arise in the task of translating a policy of this kind into reality, the reluctance of other powers to accept their share of the burdens and, linked with it, the weakness of United Nations procedures. Only a few states, perhaps a dozen all told, have the economic and military strength to take a major share in peace-keeping duties around the world. The Cold War splits some of them from the others. Some of those in Europe whose empires have died hard are still licking their wounds and for the moment want no new responsibilities overseas. The major defeated powers of the Second World

War, Japan and Germany, are both anxious to avoid any controversial interventions which might interfere with the slow process of their international rehabilitation. Countries which have recently gained their independence, while ready, as was demonstrated in the Congo, to participate in collective actions, are suspicious of being used to support what often seems to them either a Cold War objective or an attempt by an ex-imperial power to cling on to its established privileges.

To list these difficulties is simply to illustrate the obvious point that an effective international security system, whether under the United Nations or any other label, still remains to be built. It does not prove that it is not possible to do so or that a start should not be made now. Indeed, many of the obstacles mentioned can already be seen to be losing some of their obstructive power, as the Second World War passes into history and as the newly independent countries become more concerned with their international future than with disengagement from their colonial past. It cannot be too often repeated that the experience of the 1940s and 1950s is likely to be a poor guide, in these respects at least, to the realities of the 1960s and 1970s. While it may perhaps be premature to look for a corresponding transformation of Cold War pressures, these too are obviously changing and, with each year that passes, seem likely to be more firmly kept within manageable limits, so far as tacit agreement between the Soviet Union and the United States can do this.

When one adds to this the growing appreciation that significant disarmament depends upon the creation of international authority, one may be justified in thinking that the moment has now come when a new security system can be made to rise slowly out of the ashes of the old. Among the medium powers, the long-standing champions of collective security, notably the Scandinavian countries and

Canada, are more active than ever; Japan is tentatively showing that she would prefer to exert her newly-recovered influence as a major power by participation in international organizations rather than by playing a national hand in the Far East; while Germany, though kept out of the United Nations for very special reasons, recently offered a financial contribution to the United Nations operation in Cyprus. What is now needed to shift this process into a higher gear is the open and consistent support of the former imperial powers, especially Britain, which have so far been inhibited from giving it fully for fear of introducing confusion into the delicate tasks of decolonization.

We are now very near the end of this particular road and the inhibitions should be discarded. Already the acceptance by the British government of United Nations observers in North Borneo before independence and of a United Nations force in Cyprus show how far official thinking has moved over what, only ten years ago, would have been regarded as purely British responsibilities. In Southern Africa it would be wise to forestall trouble, for instance in the High Commission Territories, by associating the United Nations at an early stage with British policies, instead of waiting until a crisis has arisen. In this way international pressures can perhaps be built up which make the eventual danger of resort to force less likely.

It is no use pretending, however, that a system of this kind can be immediately effective in all conditions. It still has to be built. Moreover, where the Cold War is directly involved or where a fighting rather than a peacekeeping force is required, the United Nations Organization is still manifestly unable to take the first strain. For reasons already mentioned, serious fighting situations are perhaps less likely to be allowed to develop in future than they have been in the past, but provision has to be made for them. For the time being this can be done only by the few powers which have the capacity, and Britain is prominent among them.

No doubt this was in Harold Wilson's mind when he defined Britain's future role in terms of defence[5] as one of 'putting out brush fires all over the world', adding that 'our Commonwealth associations and naval tradition will enable us to play a big part in stopping big wars'. There is everything to be said for Britain taking her share in mutual defence arrangements, which are likely to remain a feature of the world order for some time to come, but she should accept responsibilities only for valid contemporary reasons and only for limited periods of time. She should not, in pursuance of some lingering concept of a Pax Britannica, claim to have a unique role or involve herself in open-ended treaties which, like her existing agreements in Arabia, compel her to carry over the obligations of one decade or even century into the wholly different conditions of the next.

It is impossible to foresee how soon a policy of this kind would operate to effect major changes in Britain's overseas role. In the Middle East the time required might be short. In South East Asia the process would be slower. There might for some years be little saving in the defence budget. But however long it might take to implement, it would begin at once to affect Britain's own attitude to her world role and consequently to her relations with other powers. It would, for instance, save her from futile and possibly disruptive feelings of indignation if, as suggested earlier, she finds that even her Commonwealth colleagues feel obliged gradually to dissociate themselves from her in South East Asia. It could undoubtedly ease her diplomatic position in the United Nations and make her more accept-

[5] Interview on Independent Television, reported in *The Times*, 27 Apr. 1964.

able as a contributor to United Nations forces than she has so far been. Finally, it would enable the British people to see themselves more nearly as they are already seen by others, as a major secondary power, sharing interests around the world with all other industrial trading nations, but no longer singled out from them by virtue of the military or naval functions which, as we have seen, she sometimes purports to exercise on their behalf. Such a change of attitude would also help Britain to strike the right balance in dividing her own efforts between world strategy and world trade and to consider more dispassionately and with less mysticism where, in her relationships with Europe and with the Commonwealth, reality is in future to be found.

5

Britain in World Trade

So FAR attention has been focused upon problems of strategy and on their political implications. It has been argued that it is in Britain's interests to promote the solidarity of the West as a whole, for purposes both of defence and of the conduct of East-West relations, and to encourage the replacement of Empire by a more modern system of world-wide collective security. It has been a further contention that, at least in the strategic field, Britain's appropriate place within the Western alliance lies at the European end of the Atlantic partnership; while her other overseas responsibilities, though still substantial, will not in future be such as to single her out as a special kind of power, playing a wholly different part in the world from other industrial powers of her size in Europe or elsewhere.

The question must now be asked whether economic considerations point in the same or in another direction and what are their political consequences. Britain's Empire was based upon a combination of trade and military control and it would not be surprising to find that the pattern of British trade today, as of British military dispositions, still bears some signs of having been formed in conditions very different from those of today and that there are established interests in Britain for which the necessary adjustment to change is painful. Britain's economic system has shown itself more flexible than some of her military dispositions, because her trade was never wholly geared to her imperial power. Nevertheless the old slogan

Britain in World Trade

'trade follows the flag' had a basis in reality and the withdrawal of the flag from so many parts of the world inevitably has commercial consequences.

The objective of multilateral trade

There is fortunately no need to become sentimental about those features of the Empire which embodied formal preferences for Britain's trade with her dependencies. For these were never elevated into a comprehensive system and are in any case of quite recent origin. Of course, the fact of British administration, the use of the English language, and the prevalence of British trading and governmental methods gave British traders a flying start all over the Empire, but formal discrimination was not the rule. Britain's interest as a world-wide trader, who enjoyed for many decades a technological lead over most rivals, lay overwhelmingly in promoting a free system of multilateral trade, and, by and large, she applied this throughout her own dominions. It was not until the Ottawa agreements of 1932 that substantial preferences were introduced, and it took a catastrophic breakdown in world trade to bring this about. Since then, the force of the agreements has been whittled away rather than developed, so that by the mid-1950s the margin of Commonwealth preference was on average only half as great as it had been twenty years before. This process has continued and only another world slump would be likely to reverse the trend, by forcing desperate governments back to narrow economic nationalism. Such a development would certainly not be confined to the Commonwealth and, cumulatively, would add up to a world disaster, bringing with it incalculable political repercussions.

This is not to say that world-wide free trade is either a possible or a desirable objective of British policy. In almost all countries, government intervention in economic affairs at home is now too firmly established to allow of the application of *laissez-faire* principles to international trade. Moreover free trade favours the economically strong. It would have no chance of international acceptance in a world which gives so much political weight to economically weak states, whose drive to develop new industries as a basis for the modernization of the social structure may often require them to take protective measures against industrially advanced rivals.

What can, however, be said is that Britain's interests are still best served by a widely based system of multilateral trade, embodying as few obstacles as possible to the free interchange of goods, especially between economically advanced communities. Substantial departures from this general concept will no doubt have to be accepted, but should be recognized as exceptions. The aim should be to keep them to a minimum, except where, on balance, they will tend to increase international trade in the long run, for instance by promoting development which would not otherwise occur. They should not be encouraged when their object is to enable a particular power to maintain a privileged position in a selected market or, more crudely still, to protect high-cost industry in a developed country.

EEC and the Kennedy round

If this overall attitude to trade is accepted, then GATT, whatever its detailed imperfections, is probably the best available international instrument for Britain's purposes and it will be in Britain's interest to work within its rules. Even if Britain were herself to become a member of the European Economic Community, which has a large internal free market, membership of GATT would still be in her interest. So long as this is not the case, freedom to compete on reasonably equal terms with others in all world markets is vital to her. This has, broadly, been her attitude in recent years, but her policy of pursuing a multilateral, non-discriminatory, low-tariff trading system, like the 'three overlapping circles' in the political field, was until recently, seen as rather a distant goal calling for no very drastic adjustments of her own established practices. What turned the general concept into an urgent practical issue was the action of her six European neighbours in deciding to discriminate in favour of one another and against the outside world by organizing themselves into a customs union. This gave Britain a strong incentive either to join the customs union envisaged by the Six or, if she remained outside, to make a serious effort to secure the reduction of the common tariff, which was about to be operated against her.

After a vain attempt in 1958 to find an intermediate solution by creating a free trade area with the Six, the British government eventually decided to attempt both these remedies simultaneously, by applying to join the European Economic Community and by lending its support to the United States' initiative, embodied in the Kennedy round, for a dramatic all-round reduction in the tariffs of industrial countries. The attempt to join the Common Market having been frustrated in early 1963, the reduction of the common external tariff became doubly important. The failure to enlarge the EEC removed the more dramatic possibilities of the Kennedy round, since the domestic trade legislation of the United States had been designed to permit more drastic tariff reductions with the enlarged Community. Nevertheless the reductions still practicable are sufficient to lift the process of tariff reduction to a new level of effectiveness. In any event, the Kennedy round is to be seen as only the beginning of a continuing process which it should be Britain's object to support, offering concessions in her own preferential system as an inducement to others to co-operate in eliminating obstacles to multilateral trade.

EFTA

Another result of the Brussels breakdown was to give a new lease of life to EFTA, a body which had been somewhat unloved from its birth in 1959. During the negotiations the interests of EFTA, though constantly referred to, were inevitably given a rather low priority, since, if Britain had secured entry to EEC, at least two of her EFTA partners, Denmark and Norway, would almost certainly have entered with her, while a third, Austria, would have sought association with the enlarged Community. EFTA would thus have disintegrated, leaving its remaining members to make such terms as they could to safeguard their European trade. This apparently cavalier treatment could be justified by the fact that, when EFTA was formed, it had been seen by most of its members as a means of coming to terms with EEC rather than as a permanent rival trading group. Moreover its members had not, at the time of the Brussels negotiations, begun to take action on the basis of their EFTA obligations, on a scale which could have given them strong moral grounds for demanding the continuance of the partnership.

The Brussels breakdown preserved EFTA's identity and made it seem somewhat less ephemeral. It also led to a decision, at the Lisbon meeting in May 1963, to accelerate the earlier timetable in such a way as to complete the free trade area for industrial products, subject to a few exceptions for Norway and a general exception for Portugal, by the end of 1966. This means that, within two or three years, EFTA will have taken collective action of a substantial kind and will thereby have created a range of mutual obligations among its members, which must surely compel greater respect for their interests in any future European negotiation than it was able to secure between August 1961 and January 1963. The question therefore arises whether EFTA ought now to be considered as a longer-lasting institution and, if so, whether some further use can be made of it beyond what is already envisaged.

The most obvious course for consideration is to turn EFTA into a customs union, which would involve creating a common external tariff for the Seven and would result in the members developing a common commercial policy and bargaining collectively as a unit with third parties. It is, however, doubtful whether there is a basis for a mutually acceptable arrangement of this kind. The Swiss and Swedes, for instance, are not keen to raise their external tariffs, which are lower than those of either the Six or Britain. They would probably have been prepared to do so, though reluctantly, when the reward was to be access to the markets of the Six as well as the British market. Without this prospect they have little incentive, since they already have favourable access to the British market on account of the free trade area. Even if Britain were to agree that the tariffs should be harmonized at their level, the gain for the Swiss and the Swedes would be doubtful, for where Britain reduced her most-favoured-nation tariffs they would actually lose some of the margin of preference they now enjoy over other suppliers.

In any case Britain would not find sufficient advantage in harmonizing at the Swiss-Swedish level to compensate her for having to apply the Seven's common tariff against the Commonwealth. Moreover the reduction in her own moderately high tariff would reduce her bargaining power in dealing with other countries. These difficulties simply reflect the fact that the members of EFTA have such widely differing interests that the highest common factor which can be found among them is too low to offer really worth-while possibilities of common action. EFTA's future depends largely upon the way in which the external trading policies of EEC evolve. While this remains uncertain, EFTA can provide useful machinery for promoting trade and concerting policy among the principal countries of Western Europe which are left outside the EEC, but the possibilities for further development do not go much beyond this. EFTA certainly does not seem to offer to Britain opportunities which could prove more than marginal in planning the pattern for her future world trade.

Effects of the Brussels negotiations

It would be unrewarding now to rehearse in detail all the arguments so hotly debated during the period of the Brussels negotiations, when Britain's trading partners, inside and outside the Commonwealth, were trying to assess the consequences for them of Britain becoming part of a European Common Market. But the failure of the negotiations did not restore the previous position and most of the issues, which these negotiations raised, still have to be faced in one form or another.

The possibility of British entry into EEC, for instance, threatened existing Commonwealth preferences in a particularly sharp way, because it would have involved not only their abolition, but their replacement by the granting to Britain's European partners of preferential entry into the British market on terms not open to the Commonwealth. Much British effort was expended in an effort to cushion the transition from one system to another and to spread it over a reasonable period, but the end result of the process was never in doubt. It would, in effect, have been, in the phrase used by critics at the time,

'Commonwealth preference in reverse'. The question was therefore raised for Britain's Commonwealth trading partners whether they should not concentrate upon recouping their seemingly inevitable losses in the British market by developing their trade with other industrial countries.

In the case of some Commonwealth countries in Africa, this question arose in a particularly acute form because their trade was threatened whether Britain joined EEC or not. If she joined, they would lose the preferential treatment they enjoyed in the United Kingdom market and would obtain compensatory access to the market of EEC only if they accepted associated status under the Rome Treaty. This they were mostly reluctant to do for political reasons. If on the other hand Britain did not join EEC, they still faced losses of a different kind, because the preferences, which their trading rivals in French-speaking Africa had previously enjoyed in the French market only, were due to be extended to the whole of the EEC market, to which some Commonwealth countries had been accustomed to export on equal terms. In the event, when Britain did not join EEC, the Commonwealth countries were left to make their own deal with Brussels as best they could.

Finally, the mere fact of the British application of 1961 was sufficient to raise in the minds of all the countries which had traditionally relied upon the British market the question of the future strength of the British economy. The switch in British policy had been sharp and was made with little preparation of the public mind either at home or abroad, so that it seemed a fair inference that the government had concluded that Britain could not maintain her industrial and commercial position if she remained outside EEC. This question was, of course, hotly disputed within Britain and the inference was strongly denied by those who opposed British integration with Europe. But the trains of thought which had been started could not be suddenly stopped when the Brussels negotiations ended.

Indeed, of all the issues raised by the application of 1961, the only one which ended with the negotiations in January 1963 was the immediate prospect of 'Commonwealth preference in reverse'. But the whittling away of Commonwealth preferences, the drive by Commonwealth countries to diversify their trade in industrial markets other than the United Kingdom, the need for tropical countries in Africa to come to terms with EEC, and the question-mark hanging over the future economic strength of Britain—all these have so entered the consciousness of the world trading community as to seem irreversible.

There is evidence of this available under each of the headings. In the international trade discussions of 1964 not only Britain but other Commonwealth countries too made it clear that the Ottawa preferences are not sacrosanct but are negotiable in return for concessions. Several Commonwealth countries are continuing on their own account the negotiations for better access to the market of EEC, which Britain initiated on their behalf in Brussels. At least one country of tropical Africa, Nigeria, is among them. Australia and New Zealand are increasing their trade with Japan. Most Commonwealth countries have been demonstrating their positive support for multilateralism in the Kennedy round and in the United Nations Conference on Trade and Development. Even if Ottawa preferences still linger on, the spirit of Ottawa is dead. The doubt about Britain's continuing ability to provide by herself adequate financial and industrial backing for the needs of so varied a group of less developed economies has contributed to the relative depreciation of what was in the past an essentially London-centred concept.

These post-Brussels developments are already sufficient to show that the sharp distinction which was drawn at the height of the controversy over Britain's relations with Europe, between Britain joining a 'rich man's club' on the one hand and leading a Commonwealth partnership comprising developed and less developed countries on the other, was at best an over-simplification. However true it may be that some Commonwealth countries would have suffered immediate disadvantage from Britain's adoption of the common external tariff and the common agricultural policy of the Six, it is now clear that the older system was in any case in sharp decline. What is now needed is to establish a sound relationship between the more and the less developed areas of the world, between North and South generally, and not the continuance in the commercial field of the discriminatory linking of particular industrial countries with areas once under their imperial control. If this is right, not only is Commonwealth preference obsolescent, but the correctness of the EEC's system of association with French-speaking Africa is also open to question. In the long run the right solution is more likely to be found in some arrangement which regulates the relations between developing and developed countries generally than in a strengthening of this aspect of either the Commonwealth or the EEC systems.

Britain and the Commonwealth

To assert that the Ottawa agreements have been losing their force and that no future system of trade can be built upon them is not to denigrate the immense importance to Britain of her trade with Commonwealth countries. Britain's exports to these countries in each of the years

1959–63 have topped £100 million per month (except in 1962 when they were £99·2 million), a figure which is roughly a third of her exports to the whole world. The high proportion of their total imports which these countries take from Britain has been dropping for the past ten years, as the diversification of the trade of Commonwealth countries proceeds. The drop may also reflect a certain failure by Britain to modernize her own economy and to adapt herself to the needs of countries which are no longer under her direct control. Nevertheless the quantity of British trade which flows through these channels is impressive, and there is every reason why Britain should seek to keep it so.

She has a number of natural assets which should enable her to do this. Established connexions, common language, and mutual familiarity all give her an advantage over competitors in Commonwealth markets. But any attempt to add institutional to natural advantages would be doomed to failure for want of a sufficient common interest among the widely varied countries of the Commonwealth. Not only are these countries unwilling to form a free trade area or customs union with the United Kingdom but, as Sir Alec Douglas-Home explained in Parliament,[1] even the formation of a Commonwealth Economic Development Council is acceptable to them only on condition that it is a purely consultative body without executive powers. This attitude is a natural consequence of their growing desire to diversify their trade, which received additional impetus from Britain's application to join the EEC.

Britain can hope to remain a substantial exporter to Commonwealth countries and a substantial market for their produce and will also, no doubt, continue to be a supplier to them of capital and technical assistance. But

[1] 6 Feb. 1964, H. C. Deb., vol. 688, col. 1359.

she is not likely to find in the Commonwealth a willingness to buy special privileges in the British market by means either of formal arrangements which would be in conflict with GATT rules, or of informal 'Buy British' practices which would cause difficulties for them with other potential suppliers. Even from the United Kingdom's point of view the apparent attractions of a 'Buy British' policy within the Commonwealth are deceptive. As a world trading nation Britain would probably be better advised to concentrate on resisting 'Buy American' policies in all markets than to imitate them in a limited number of territories with which she herself has historic connexions.

Similarly, it seems doubtful wisdom for Britain to try to make the provision of capital or technical assistance to developing Commonwealth countries conditional upon special trading arrangements. A system of this kind does not suit developing countries, which need a balanced programme of development and not one distorted by a series of deals. Nor is it in Britain's interest to see the world divided up by the developed countries into exclusive spheres of interest, whether these are based upon former imperial connexions or upon newly negotiated commercial ties.

The conclusion must be that the advantages which Britain enjoys in Commonwealth countries will in future depend upon her preserving, in a new world of competitive multilateral trading, the relationship of trust and intimacy which she built up in the past, and not upon organized discrimination. The scope for basing special trading arrangements upon the Commonwealth connexion is likely to be narrow, because Britain and the other Commonwealth countries alike have a long-term interest in promoting multilateral trade. For this concept, the future commercial policy of EEC is of great importance, whether Britain joins it or not, and both Britain and the

Commonwealth would be wise to concentrate upon enlisting the co-operation of EEC in multilateral practices rather than themselves adopting discriminatory devices, which would be likely to encourage similar attitudes in Europe and incidentally in the United States. This approach has the further advantage, in terms of British politics, that it would allow a common attitude to Britain's trade to be shared both by those who believe that Britain's eventual destiny lies with Europe and those who do not, and would enable British traders and industrialists to make long-term plans without the fear of sharp reversals of commercial policy whenever government changes.

The role of sterling

It is in keeping with the policy of supporting widely-based multilateral trading arrangements that Britain should be prepared to take a fresh look at the role of sterling as a world currency. That sterling still is acceptable to foreign governments is shown by the fact that more than 10 per cent of the world's official currency reserves are held in sterling. At a time when it is widely asserted that international liquidity is becoming inadequate for the needs of world trade, sterling's role as a key currency could scarcely be reduced, unless there was fair assurance that something better was ready to take its place.

Yet there are at least two major reasons for doubting whether the present system should be maintained for much longer unaltered. The first reason concerns the effect on the British economy. Britain's balance of payments has been a continual source of worry since 1945. Even at the best of times she has been able to achieve only an exiguous current-account surplus and, at less favourable moments, has found herself compelled in consequence to adopt policies which have repeatedly checked her economic growth. On these occasions the fact that she runs an international reserve currency puts Britain in a particularly exposed position, because large foreign holdings are liable to be turned in, with the resulting risk that her reserves will run down faster than would be the case with an ordinary currency. Britain's sterling reserves have more than once proved inadequate to withstand this strain except at the cost of the abandonment of domestic policies which, but for sterling's special position, would be perfectly sound.

As against this, it is often claimed that Britain's export trade derives advantages from the special facilities which she is able to offer by reason of her management of a great reserve currency; and, further, that the services provided by the City of London bring in a substantial quantity of foreign exchange, to the benefit of Britain's balance of payments. A comparison of the recent performance of British exports with those of countries which do not run a reserve currency goes far to dispose of the first point; while, on the second, the foreign-exchange earnings clearly attributable to sterling's key role are equivalent only to some 2–3 per cent of the country's normal exports of merchandise. It is at least doubtful whether such gains can compensate Britain for the exceptional caution which the management of sterling imposes upon her in the expansion of her own economy.

The second reason for doubt concerns sterling's contribution to meeting the world's demand for additional liquidity. If a national currency like sterling is used to increase the currency reserves of other countries, and thus make them more liquid, this must mean that the rest of the world is in one way or another requiring more sterling than it is spending. In other words the British balance of payments is in overall deficit. But after a time the piling up of deficits in this way brings the currency itself under suspicion, so that foreigners are reluctant to hold it and it loses much of its value as a source of international liquidity. The argument applies in the long run to the dollar as much as to the pound sterling. What is needed here is a much more broadly-based system than Britain or indeed any one country can provide on its own, and this would require a major collective act of credit creation on the part of creditor nations. If Britain had entered EEC in 1963, one result would probably have been increased co-operation between sterling and the European currencies and probably an eventual merging of them all. As it is, various attempts by Britain to obtain international backing for sterling have encountered suspicion on the part of creditor countries, though there is already evidence of a growing readiness both in Europe and in the United States to develop techniques for the mutual support of currencies both through the International Monetary Fund and on a bilateral basis.

It is not intended to enter into the jungle of technical argument which surrounds the currency problem.[2] All that is necessary here is to make the point that Britain should not be misled by proud statements, however true, that some 40 per cent of the world's trade is conducted in sterling into assuming that this necessarily brings her either economic gain or greater national freedom of action. The contrary is more probably true. As with her overseas military commitments already discussed, so with her sterling obligations, the remedy is not to retire into a small national shell, but rather to take a fair share in a multilateral system designed for the second half of the twentieth century. The creation of such a system is not an easy operation and, like the building of a military security system, involves an awkward transitional phase in which

---

[2] For more detailed discussion see Christopher McMahon, *Sterling in the Sixties* (1964). (Chatham House Essay.)

there could be a failure of confidence both in the old and the new methods. This is a good reason for approaching the operation cautiously, and seeking to secure the underpinning of sterling by co-operative international measures as a first step. It is not a good reason for Britain maintaining the thesis that her currency's time-honoured role must be maintained intact, both for the sake of her own economic greatness and as a service to the world. The truth is that something new is needed for both purposes, and Britain should make it an object of her policy to organize the change.

6

The Options Open to Britain

THE ending of the Brussels negotiations in January 1963 put an end for the time being to Britain's attempt to join the EEC. This attempt, begun in 1961, had involved a striking departure from the declared attitude of both the main British political parties, and so little had been done in advance to prepare either British or Continental opinion for the change that, in retrospect, the whole episode bears the appearance of a gambler's throw. It may well have been the right thing to do, it was skilfully conducted and it might have come off. But in the event it failed and it cannot be repeated in precisely this form again.

The ending of the negotiations did not settle for Britain the principal questions which the signature of the Treaty of Rome had raised. All it did was to close, for the time being, one particular avenue of approach to problems which still remain to be solved. It left Britain as divided as ever on the question whether this avenue had been the right one and should consequently be tried again later on, or whether it was a dead end.

Must Britain integrate?

Two issues in particular, which figured prominently in the thinking of those who decided to open the negotiations in 1961, still call for discussion. Firstly, in the new era of giant states, is it necessary for Britain to contemplate integrating herself economically, and eventually politically, with others, surrendering national sovereignty so as to form part of a greater whole? If the answer is yes, Western Europe provides the only available group for the purpose. Secondly, since integration with Europe is in any case not immediately possible, and cannot now be assumed to be possible even in the long run, Britain still faces the older question of her relations with Western Europe. In the past Britain's main objective was always to prevent the emergence of a single overwhelmingly powerful state on the Continent. This policy is now obsolete on at least two counts. Firstly, the relevant balance of power is no longer a purely European one but affects the whole world; and secondly, the prevention of further conflict within Western Europe is now just as essential to Britain as to France and Germany. Britain's interest is, therefore, no longer to obstruct the unity of Western Europe but to exert some influence upon its evolution and upon its eventual impact in world affairs. This is equally inescapable whether Britain becomes integrated with the Continent or remains outside.

It has already been observed that various circumstances have delayed for a generation or more the consequences to Britain of the emergence of advanced industrial powers far larger than herself in area, population, and resources. The delay is now at an end and certain choices have to be made. It is no doubt true that a skilled nation of 50 million people is still large enough to engage successfully in most of the activities of a sovereign state, subject to making reasonable arrangements with others for collective defence. But already there are some industrial and scientific fields in which no power the size of Britain can any longer compete with larger rivals. Modern armaments is one, space research another, supersonic civil aircraft probably a third, and there now seems to be doubt about nuclear power. In civilian industry a solution may be found simply by collaboration between two or more independent medium-sized states, as in the case of the Anglo-French Concorde aircraft, though in future this type of agreement will probably be more often made inside the Community than with outsiders.

Where defence is involved, permanent dependence upon another power for the manufacture and supply of essential armaments is more serious, since it carries with it the implication of reduced national freedom of action in foreign policy and reduced influence in the world. Britain has, of course, been dependent for more than a hundred years on outside sources for at least one essential requirement of national survival, food. During most of the period the disadvantages of this have been minimized by her control of the seas and of primary-producing territories around the world, though even so it became a serious source of weakness in both world wars. What would be new to Britain would be to find that, on grounds of size alone, she was no longer able in peacetime to compete, over the whole field of industrial production, with larger economies such as the United States and the Soviet Union. If to these existing giants there were to be added a powerful Western European union, it is obvious that, with China and others looming just off-stage, Britain could no longer claim to be in the top rank of world powers.

This is not to say that she could not be prosperous. A medium-sized, or even a small but advanced industrial power which is prepared to specialize may compete economically with larger economies and maintain a high standard of living. Sweden and Switzerland are there to prove it. But only a large economy with a large assured market can hope to maintain the necessary specialization in all fields. For this purpose an economy of 50 million people is now becoming somewhat too small. As yet there may be only a few industries which are beyond the power of Britain to operate on her own, but these are already significant enough to have raised doubts, for instance, about British ability to compete in third markets with European industry once the Common Market is fully established. Even in the short period since the end of the Brussels negotiations in 1963 it can be seen that size and power are beginning to tell against Britain in international politics, for instance in the weight given to EEC in the Kennedy round and in the determination of the United States to proceed, along with Germany and Italy, in evolving the mixed-manned force in NATO, irrespective of Britain's willingness to participate, provided that the scheme has sufficient support in Europe.

Opponents of British integration with Europe often attack it on the ground that it would involve surrender of sovereignty, but this approach is of little assistance in dealing with the British problem. Sovereignty in the juridical sense loses much of its value if it does not in practice give a nation control over its own affairs, and the fact is that neither Britain nor any of the larger powers of Europe can now have the kind of national control of their affairs which they enjoyed in the past. In major military and economic policies they have only the choice between two alternative forms of dependence. They can either maintain formal sovereignty, while remaining none the less dependent, as smaller nations have always been, on the decisions of larger powers; or they can join together in pooling their sovereignty with others so as to form a bigger political unit, strong enough to be a great power in modern conditions and to enjoy something like the freedom of action which was available to them as separate nation-states in the past.

Britain and EEC

The countries of Western Europe, in signing the Treaty of Rome, clearly chose to attempt the second alternative. How soon or how completely they will achieve it remains to be seen. Britain's somewhat hectic attempt to join them in this enterprise having been frustrated, at least for the time being, she now has to think again. She has not clearly made up her mind on what she wants, nor is it now certain when or even whether the choice of joining EEC will again be open to her. Whatever the outcome of this debate, there can be no doubt of the interest which Britain has in finding a way of retaining some influence upon the political and economic evolution of her European neighbours.

'Before proposing the revolutionary merger of the British economy into EEC', wrote Nora Beloff in her account of the Brussels negotiations,[1] 'Britain should perhaps have stopped to examine what kind of Europe she wanted and why.'[1] This examination may have been adequately made in Whitehall and among a few members of the Cabinet before August 1961, but if so the public was not taken into the government's confidence at that time. Once the lengthy negotiations had begun, it became harder for the government to talk frankly, for fear of prejudicing Edward Heath's bargaining position in Brussels.

The record of Britain's attitude to European unity throughout the post-war period and her attempt, after the Treaty of Rome had been signed, to secure a favourable economic relationship with the Community without joining it, by the creation of a wider free trade area, suggest that Britain would have preferred to avoid the question of European integration altogether. A further evolution of the sort of inter-governmental co-operation practised in

[1] Nora Beloff, *The General Says No* (Penguin Books, 1963.)

NATO and OEEC would have suited her better. Her attitude to Europe was not essentially unco-operative, but her interests were so much more varied than those of her Continental neighbours, that economic and eventually political integration into a body whose interests lay overwhelmingly in Europe simply seemed to her too difficult to contemplate. Rightly or wrongly, she could not bring herself to take the plunge, and at nearly all the crucial moments of European development up to 1957 she managed to convince herself that European unity would in any case not be achieved in the form which the Six envisaged.

There are still traces of this thinking in Britain. For some time after January 1963 it was widely believed that the Community had been brought to a standstill and might even break up under the impact of de Gaulle's single-minded nationalism. When this prospect became less likely and the Community began again to get painfully under way, it was pointed out that, economically, Britain's trade with the Six did not seem to be suffering and that in any case the political unity of the Community had probably been indefinitely postponed. There was therefore little need for Britain to do anything in particular about her relations with Europe. She should simply continue to promote her European trade and, for the rest, look to other areas around the world, as she had done so successfully in the past.

This advice does not seem likely to remain valid for long. Discrimination against British traders in the European market will become more serious in the near future. Moreover the conviction is growing in Europe that the processes which the Treaty of Rome set in motion are now irreversible. Already there are moves to strengthen the political unity of the Six in their relations with one another, by the merging of the three Communities and in other ways. The co-ordination of policy towards the outside world will certainly take longer and may not make great progress while de Gaulle is the ruler of France, for the basis of unity in this field does not yet exist. But Europeans are prepared to wait for this, and it is at least possible that, if de Gaulle were to depart within a few years, the waiting period would turn out to be shorter than is now supposed.

In any event, it would be exceedingly unwise for Britain to frame her policies now on any other assumption than that the Community will steadily consolidate itself and that at some time within the next decade a new centre of power will have been created in Western Europe, already economically formidable and with the prospect of political and strategic significance being gradually added to it.

If this is correct, then the political nature of this new giant and particularly its attitude in world affairs must be of great importance to Britain, whether she herself becomes a part of it or not. Since Britain does a substantial and increasing amount of trade with the countries of the Community, she would wish it to give her liberal access to its market with the common tariff at a low rather than a high level. Since Britain must still base her defence upon co-operation with both Europe and America, she would wish her neighbour to favour a similar system and to aim at agreeing upon common policies for the West in her relations with the Soviet bloc. Finally, since one of Britain's main preoccupations in the coming decade will be the relationship between the developed and the developing countries, she would wish for the co-operation of developed Europe, with other developed communities, in a worldwide programme of trade and aid.

Many of those who have helped to build the Community have always seen it as playing this kind of role and have

The Options Open to Britain

tended to claim that the fear of the new Europe evolving in any other direction is unreal. But in fact there have always been other tendencies present in Europe, working for a narrowly Europe-centred community, based upon largely autarchic conceptions and upon securing a measure of insulation from world competition behind a high tariff barrier. The differences rather than the similarities between Europe and North America have been emphasized and the assertion of a separate European personality has been valued more highly than Western solidarity. So far as aid to the developing world is concerned, this school of thought has confined itself fairly strictly to the maintenance of special links between the Community and those developing countries which were previously dependencies of one or other of the European powers.

Throughout the Community's earlier years, this tendency was partly a natural defensive reaction by countries which were engaged upon an exceedingly difficult enterprise and required to develop a sense of separateness from others in order to emphasize their own unity. It was indeed an essential feature of the whole undertaking that the Community should grow out of a combination of a common market formed among its members and a common tariff barrier separating them from everyone else. This was not an unreasonable device and was perfectly consistent with an intention, as soon as the community had become established, to shift to more broadly conceived policies and a wider world outlook. A measure of self-absorption, sometimes amounting to isolationism, has, after all, been a familiar feature of many great communities, which have had to conquer their own internal divisions first, before becoming citizens of the world.

By 1961, a period of high confidence in the Community, there were numerous signs that the sensational recovery in the economic strength of the Six was already creating a more 'outward-looking' mentality. Certainly one of the aims of those Europeans who favoured Britain's entry into EEC was to reinforce this trend by the inclusion of new members, whose national interests drew them into the 'outward-looking' camp. But by this time the issue had become complicated by the impact of de Gaulle who, for the time being at least, had his own reasons for wishing to see the Community take another course.

De Gaulle's view of Europe

Much of de Gaulle's motivation is widely shared in Europe. His desire to assert Europe's renewed status in the world; his conviction that independent nuclear armaments are an essential element in this status; his emphasis upon Franco-German co-operation as a basis for European unity and the priority which he gives to this over European-American co-operation within an Atlantic framework, in all this de Gaulle is a representative European figure. If he were to disappear from the political scene, there would be many others to voice the same views, and indeed to feel the same doubts which de Gaulle has so forcibly expressed about Britain's readiness to join fully in the enterprise of building united Europe. Britain must beware of attributing to de Gaulle alone the difficulties which she has encountered in Europe. Undoubtedly the aggressiveness of his diplomatic technique has given a cutting edge to European arguments which might otherwise have been successfully talked away; but it may in the long run be no bad thing for Britain to have been forced, as she now is, to define much more sharply than she has yet done the place which she seeks to occupy on the European and Atlantic scene.

Unfortunately the evidence of 1963 and 1964 suggests that de Gaulle's idiosyncratic attitude to European and

Atlantic affairs includes other features which are more dangerous. Although he poses as a loyal European when he is dealing with non-Europeans, especially the United States, within Europe his purpose is the assertion of France, not the building of wider unity. In so far as an united Europe has a part in his plans, it will have to be based upon acceptance of French leadership and not upon the sharing of responsibilities by the development of community institutions. Even the Franco-German Treaty of 1963, upon whose effectiveness Gaullist policies seemed for a time to be founded, has been roughly handled by de Gaulle from the start. Whenever he has wished to pursue policies on which German agreement seemed doubtful, he has ignored the treaty provisions for consultation and has presented his ally with a *fait accompli*. Indeed he seems to be turning Laval's wartime policy inside out and offering to Germany and the other members of the Community not a genuine partnership but a place in France's new order in Europe. The clearest sign of this is his insistence that greatness is dependent upon the possession of a strategic nuclear force and that the force which he is building up is an exclusively French one, in whose formation and operation the rest of Europe is offered no share. On account of his attitude to NATO, the French force is already more inaccessible to European influence than Britain's V-bombers.

In his economic policies his objectives again seem strictly national, though he has been careful not to press them so hard as to forfeit the co-operation of his European partners in agricultural policy or to risk a break with them over the tariff negotiations of the GATT. It can be fairly said that he has shown his dislike and distrust of all forms of international co-operation, whether on a European basis in the Six, or an Atlantic basis in NATO, or in the even wider field of peace-keeping through the United

Nations. He has made it clear that, for him, the nation-state, so far from being transcended, remains for the foreseeable future the kernel of political life and that independence is, today as in the nineteenth and in earlier centuries, the essential badge of nationhood. This, he insists, is what France must claim for herself. To what extent this attitude is a permanent one and to what extent a temporary tactic, designed to restore to France, and possibly through her to Europe, some of the self-confidence which was destroyed by the disasters of the last twenty years is perhaps open to argument, for de Gaulle's policies have been readily switched on more than one occasion since 1958, when he found that they no longer paid. But so long as his present attitude is maintained there does not seem, for Britain at least, to be any possibility of compromise with it. The only course is to oppose it, with whatever means may be available, in the belief that it represents a fundamentally anachronistic and sterile view of the interests of France, of the West, and of the world, and that, although in the long run it probably cannot succeed, it is capable, before it has run its course, of undoing much of the progress in international co-operation which has been achieved since the Second World War.

There are two main fields in which the evolution of such a Europe might have dangerous consequences, firstly in the revival of nationalism within Western Europe, and secondly in the estrangement of Western Europe from North America.

The revival of nationalism

The kernel of the first of these is the relationship between France and Germany. Much of the effort of postwar German governments has been devoted to the restoration of German self-confidence on the basis not of German nationalism but of the German contribution to a larger Western European community. De Gaulle has earned immediate acclaim from German crowds by his references to them as a great people but he has placed a time-bomb under the Franco-German relationship by his insistence that the future lies with the nation-state and not with any wider community. When he asserts that ideologies are transient but the nation is permanent, he is in effect asserting the primacy of nationalism as an ideology. If this is valid doctrine for France, then it should be valid for Germany too. Up to a point de Gaulle has been willing to admit this, for instance by saying, when challenged, that the development by Germany of her own independent strategic nuclear deterrent is a question for her to decide.

This is, on the face of it, straightforward enough, even if others may think that it oversimplifies the problems which independent German nuclear armaments would raise. But the straightforwardness is belied by other aspects of de Gaulle's policy of which Germans are becoming increasingly aware. On the one hand he adopts a 'hard' attitude on Berlin, which costs France nothing and helps him in his immediate objective of separating France from supposed United States and 'Anglo-Saxon' policies. On the other hand his fixation on French national grandeur and leadership in Europe effectively rules out, if only by implication, French acceptance of a reunified Germany, whose weight in Western Europe would put France decisively in second place. Indeed, the only conditions in which German reunification could conceivably be made consistent with Gaullist ambitions for France would be a revival of the pre-war agreement between France, the Soviet Union, and Eastern Europe to keep united Germany in her place. Short of this eventuality, which is at best a rather distant prospect, de Gaulle clearly counts on the continued truncation of Germany, combined with

France's commanding lead over Germany in nuclear weapons, to ensure French predominance in Western Europe.

This is dangerously old-fashioned thinking, closely patterned on nineteenth-century concepts of the power balance between the nation-states of Europe, and for that reason probably destined to fail. In particular it requires for its fulfilment a degree of German compliance in the early stages and of Soviet co-operation in the later stages which is unlikely to be forthcoming. The danger is therefore not so much that de Gaulle will succeed but that, in failing, he will undo the achievements of the Community without putting anything acceptable in its place, so throwing Western Europe back into the jungle of national rivalries from which it has been seeking to escape.

European-American relations

The second danger is to European-American relations. The importance of these since the war needs no stressing, and it has already been argued that, when all the changes in the world scene have been taken into account, the need to maintain the partnership in some form remains. The acceptance by her allies of the predominant power of the United States was bound to become harder as Europe recovered its prosperity and self-confidence. But it is necessary, because this inequality within the alliance is a fact and nothing in the military or economic progress of Europe suggests that it will shortly cease to be a fact. This is widely recognized by the governments involved, and there are public statements by de Gaulle which show that he is no exception. The difference between him and all the other Western leaders concerns the way in which this apparently permanent imbalance should be handled. All the partners of the United States other than de Gaulle are pressing for adjustments in the framework of an alliance which will give them a more effective voice in the framing of joint policies. This phase is still in its early stages, and the question how far the United States will be willing to go in limiting her freedom of action for the sake of allied co-operation is still an open one. But given the assumption on both sides that a common interest in co-operation still exists, there is no reason for pessimism about the evolution of an arrangement reasonably well suited to the conditions of the next decade. If, in addition, something like a European 'pillar' could be built, the inequality of the two sides of the alliance could at least be reduced to more tolerable proportions.

Only de Gaulle reacts to the undoubted need for changes by stressing not common interest but divergent interest, not improved consultation but greater separatism, not the pooling of resources for joint purposes but their disentanglement from one another for the exploitation of distinct and often conflicting aims. This policy can be readily enough explained by recalling de Gaulle's hatred of the United States, arising from his treatment by President Roosevelt during the Second World War, and by linking this with his well-known identification of his own person with France. But although this explains, it cannot justify. Personal hatred among political leaders is a bad basis for national policies and even more so when the cause of it is a quarter of a century out of date. But it is none the less real, and it would be foolish to expect any change so long as the head of the French government sees every exercise of American influence as an insult to himself and through him to France. Since only de Gaulle is in this situation, it is not to be expected that the other allies of the United States can make common cause with him in this respect and he has shown his awareness of this by neglecting to consult even his German ally over his new departures of policy in Latin America, South East Asia, and China or in his withdrawal of naval forces from NATO. Some at least of these policies are in themselves perfectly defensible, but their timing and the manner of their execution betrayed a specifically anti-American motivation which left France unnecessarily isolated.

Because de Gaulle's anti-Americanism, at least in its more extreme manifestation, is unacceptable to his European partners, it may well fail in the end to dominate the Community's attitude in world affairs. But, even so, it is likely to remain, so long as it lasts, an insuperable barrier to any formal association of Britain with the Six. This is both because Britain would be unwilling to identify herself finally with a Europe whose intentions in world affairs remained at best equivocal, and also because any British move towards Europe would be almost certain to meet with a rebuff from a Gaullist-led France. One of the greatest of the many uncertainties which complicate the framing of British policy at the present time is the uncertainty about the duration of de Gaulle's leadership of France and about the nature of the policies which his immediate successors will pursue. All that can be asserted with any confidence is that, whether de Gaulle goes soon or late, there will be a waiting period, perhaps lasting for several years, before Britain's eventual relationship with Europe can be clarified, and that during that period things will move on within the Community and elsewhere.

British influence in Europe

The immediate question for Britain is, therefore, not so much whether she wishes to join the Community or not, but rather whether she can do anything to persuade Europe to move in a direction which will at least enable

Britain and her Continental neighbours to trade easily with one another and to co-operate constructively in world affairs. If this is achieved, there will be a good prospect of her eventually reaching an acceptable arrangement of a more formal kind with the sort of Europe which will have emerged, and the form which the solution may then take can be left with some confidence to be decided when the time comes. It is more relevant for the moment to consider what means are available to Britain, excluded as she is from the Community, to influence the direction in which European policies evolve. Experience since January 1963 already suggests that the answer cannot be to have no clear policy and simply to wait upon events. This is a recipe for British impotence and leaves Britain standing on the sidelines while Western policies are determined by a tussle of forces inside Europe, in which a calculation of Britain's intentions towards Europe plays no part, and by a European-American dialogue which increasingly becomes a dialogue between Washington and Bonn. It has the further disadvantage that it adds to the inevitable uncertainties which already face British business in planning its long-term investment and exports, an unnecessary uncertainty about the intentions of its own government.

There seem to be two main areas in which it may be open to Britain to influence the future direction of European policy. The first concerns the organization of nuclear armaments within the Western alliance, which has already been discussed. It is only necessary here to re-emphasize the point that Britain's existing nuclear capability gives her some leverage in helping Europe to secure a reasonable share of influence over the joint nuclear policies of the West. This is a condition of the continued effectiveness of the alliance and Britain can contribute to it only by ranging herself alongside the European allies of the United States. If she makes the other choice, of continuing to claim a special relationship with the United States, not shared by others, for the purpose of maintaining a measure of independence for her own national nuclear forces, she must expect to pay the price of having no influence upon the policies of Europe. It is not likely that, at least in the longer term, this will be compensated by correspondingly greater influence in Washington.

The second area of possible British influence concerns the future balance of forces within Western Europe itself. It is not so long since Frenchmen talked of being 'afraid of being left alone in a room with the Germans', and pressed Britain to throw her weight into the European balance as a corrective. For the time being this argument is little heard, because French economic recovery, the stability of government which de Gaulle's personal leadership has provided and, no doubt, the promise of a French strategic nuclear force have combined to make the fear of German hegemony fade and to put the possibility of French hegemony in its place. To Italy and the Benelux countries neither French nor German hegemony is a welcome prospect, while a possible Franco-German dyarchy is even more alarming. They tend to feel that a stool based upon at least three major legs, of which one would be Britain, would give both greater solidity to the whole edifice and a better assurance that no one sectional interest could come to dominate the Community as a whole.

Even in Germany, where a genuine European Community based upon Franco-German co-operation, has a strong appeal and where many have feared that British participation would have disruptive consequences, there are grave doubts about the 'Europe des patries' which de Gaulle proposes. A Europe deliberately kept small in order to give it the coherence of a communal purpose is one thing; a Europe kept small because some of its members wish to impose their own national purposes upon it is quite a different proposition. To Germans, whether of the Adenauer school, or of more liberal or left-wing tendencies, who have wished to convert the old German patriotism into something larger, the possibility of renewed scope for German national action is scarcely more attractive than the alternative of domination by French policies, assuming that France remains stable and strong.

Even this assumption can be made only with reservations, for nothing is less predictable than the nature of the French regime which will succeed de Gaulle or the date at which this will occur. One does not need to be a committed advocate of Britain's entry into Europe, or even a great admirer of Britain, in order to see that the danger of a violent swing in the European balance would be reduced if Britain were in it, even if only as a dead-weight, not to be readily shifted by rapid changes of personal leadership or of doctrine. This was one of the arguments advanced by the advocates of Britain's signature of the Treaty of Rome. Now it seems certain that, if a European crisis of this kind were to occur, Britain could not at that moment be already a member of the European Community. The question is whether, notwithstanding, there is some way in which she could exert an influence upon European decisions by giving practical support to the numerous elements in Europe which share her world outlook and would welcome her initiative.

As in the case of the nuclear issue, it is hard to avoid the conclusion that the exertion of British influence in Europe will in future be possible only to the extent that Britain is willing to identify her interests with Europe's. She cannot expect to be listened to if she sees herself as some kind of outside balancing factor in a European-American equation. The preservation of European solidarity is likely to be the uppermost thought in the minds of most of Britain's European friends in any future European crisis, and only those who can be seen to be contributing to this will get a ready hearing.

What will determine Britain's power to affect events, if such a moment comes, will be a clear knowledge in Europe, not only of what Britain's political, military, and economic objectives are in the world, but also that she is willing to pursue them in partnership with Europe and, eventually, as a part of Europe. What inhibits even Britain's best friends in Europe today from giving weight to her views is their doubt about both these points, but more particularly about the second. It was recognized by everyone that clarification of the British position could hardly be expected between January 1963 and the British general election, and this period was unexpectedly prolonged. But the British-European relationship cannot be held in suspense much longer, and things will be done on both sides, acts of omission as well as of commission, which will begin to determine whether a British voice in European affairs is in future to be heard or not.

On the European side the EEC must be expected to continue to build up its institutions and its administrative practices. Since this will inevitably be done without British participation, the process is, of course, liable to make eventual assimilation of British and Continental systems harder, but there is no reason to suppose that it alone will be decisive. Moreover the precise form which this evolution takes will no doubt be somewhat affected by the extent to which the enlargement of the Community and eventual British participation are kept alive as realizable aims among members of the Six. Progress towards the political unity of EEC, in so far as it concerns the establishment of better political control over the economic activities of the bureaucracy in Brussels would, if anything, be likely to facilitate future British association. The establishment of unity in foreign policy seems farther off and, as already stated, is unlikely to make much progress until at least the manner if not the matter of French foreign policy improves.

It is rather on the British side that policies followed from the beginning of 1965 might set a trend which it would later prove beyond Britain's power to reverse. For it is Britain which has always claimed to have various major alternative choices open to her, and her immediate future policies will be taken by the rest of the world as evidence of the reality of these options and of Britain's decision about them.

The special relationship with the U.S.

England is, in effect, insular, maritime, linked through its trade, markets and food supply to very diverse and often very distant countries. Its activities are essentially industrial and commercial, and only slightly agricultural. It has, throughout its work, very marked and original customs and traditions. In short, the nature, structure and economic context of England differ profoundly from those of the other States of the Continent.

With this paragraph, taken from de Gaulle's press conference of 14 January 1963,[2] a large section of British opinion found itself in entire agreement, for it expressed perfectly what the opponents of British membership of EEC had been saying for months past. By comparison with her neighbours, Britain has for generations thought of herself as a power which was different in kind, on account of her special relationships with the scattered countries of the Commonwealth and, more recently, with the United States, and many people in Britain felt as strongly as de Gaulle that these relationships were a barrier to British

[2] U.S. Embassy, N.Y., 14 Jan. 1963, no. 185.

integration with the Community which, to borrow another phrase from de Gaulle, 'is a strictly European construction'. 'We have always been a world power', said Harold Wilson as recently as 4 March 1964. 'We should not be corralled in Europe.'[3]

There need be no dispute about the special nature of Britain's international position in the past or about its persistence, at least in modified form, up to the present time. The question is whether this will continue in the future and, if so, what the consequences are for British policy. Relations both with the United States and with the countries of the Commonwealth have been changing so fast that even the experiences of, say, ten years ago have little relevance to Britain's future problems.

So far as the United States is concerned, she had a special relationship with Britain, largely unacknowledged, throughout the nineteenth century and right up to 1939, in the sense that she owed the luxury of isolationism primarily to the assurance of British control of the seas. Since 1945 the relationship has been reversing itself, as the United States has increasingly assumed responsibilities which Britain would once have borne. Now the relationship, which still has certain special features, is between a great power, the United States, capable of intervening all over the world, and a medium power, Britain, still possessing some convenient military facilities overseas and a limited nuclear capability. Britain's nuclear contribution, whatever its other advantages may be, is not easily justified nowadays in terms of the bargaining power which it gives in Washington, where Britain's independent deterrent is acquiesced in rather than welcomed. On the other hand her power to intervene with conventional forces in some parts of the world is still useful to the United States

---

[3] Statement on return from United States, reported in *Daily Telegraph*, *Daily Express*, and other newspapers, 5 Mar. 1964.

and will probably continue to be so for some time to come. There is, however, evidence, for instance in the attitude of the United States to British action in Arabia in the spring of 1964, which suggests that American support is likely to be more readily forthcoming for British intervention if it is closely linked with up-to-date international obligations rather than with the tail-end of imperial commitments.

In the meantime other competitors for influence in Washington are appearing, Japan and Australia so far as Pacific security is concerned, and the countries of the EEC in the West. The United States has no need of British mediation in her dealings with any of these countries, whose policies are in some cases beginning to be as important to her as those of Britain. It is not sought to argue here, nor could it be reasonably argued, that these countries are today more influential in Washington than Britain, though this would probably become true of the Six countries of EEC if they were, eventually, to achieve a common foreign policy. The point is simply that the relationship with Britain, as seen from the American end, is already much less 'special' than it looks from London. This can be clearly seen by anyone who reads the major pronouncements of American Presidents on world affairs, in which Britain is seldom singled out from the other allies of the United States. The converse would not, of course, be true of pronouncements from London for, in this relationship 'Il y a toujours un qui baise et l'autre qui tend la joue.'

For almost all aspects of British policy co-operation with the United States is essential and if Britain had to make a sharp choice between her relations with the United States and her relations with any other country or group of countries she might well have to give priority to the United States. That is why it is so important to her that Europe should not evolve in a manner which faces her with a stark decision of this kind. And that is why the optimum policy for her would be one in which she ranged herself as one among several of the allies of the United States, in such a way as to ensure the wider unity of the countries on both sides of the Atlantic. To say this is not to be 'un-European', for very many Continental supporters of European unity share this aim. Indeed, it may well turn out that the only way in which the wider harmony between Europe and America can be preserved will be for Britain to assist, by identifying herself with Europe, in obtaining for the European component in the Western alliance the sort of influence in Washington without which Europeans might come to find the unequal partnership intolerable.

If the price of this is the surrender of British pretensions to special treatment in Washington, it should be paid for the sake of the greater gain, all the more since there is so little assurance that the special relationship will, in any event, be maintained much longer on the American side. It should be enough for Britain that her common language and her innumerable historical links with the United States, through family ties, educational exchanges, and the like, give her certain advantages which it is hard for other allies to share. These are likely to continue so long as she does not overplay her hand.

Relations with the Commonwealth

Britain's special relationship with the Commonwealth has to be discussed in different terms, because much more has been claimed for it and it arouses stronger emotions. Britain is still the most powerful member of the Commonwealth and, notwithstanding the size and large population of some member countries, she is likely to remain so for some time to come. The Commonwealth countries

The Options Open to Britain

have some common features as a consequence of their having once been ruled from London, but in most respects they are exceedingly diverse in their interests, in their cultural backgrounds, and in the stages they have reached in political and economic development.

The fact that all Commonwealth countries still have close links with London has tended to create in Britain an illusion, not shared elsewhere, about the extent to which the Commonwealth as a whole forms a single community. For most of the other members, the Commonwealth means their bilateral relationship with Britain. Only marginally does it involve special co-operation with other Commonwealth members, and then usually on account of regional considerations, which would have a validity of their own even if the Commonwealth did not exist. Even where regional co-operation exists, as between Australia and New Zealand, or Canada and the West Indies, it can rarely be contemplated on an exclusively Commonwealth basis. In particular the United States, as a world power with influence in almost all parts of the world, is a virtually indispensable participant even in undertakings which have a Commonwealth origin. The Colombo Plan, launched by Australia in 1950, is an example of this. Initially a Commonwealth scheme for regional aid and technical assistance, it was quickly extended to include non-Commonwealth countries at both the giving and the receiving ends. Equally in defence, it is as true for many other Commonwealth countries as it is for Britain herself that the United States link is of greater importance than any co-operation that could be devised within the Commonwealth club. Certainly few Commonwealth countries, least of all the oldest members, Canada, Australia, and New Zealand, could afford to think of Commonwealth partnership as an alternative to the American connexion, or indeed to regional co-operation.

So far as Britain is concerned, the main value of the Commonwealth lies in established trade, which has already been discussed, and in a certain ease of communication due to the personal familiarity and common forms of training which link so many of the political, military, and administrative classes in Commonwealth countries. These are assets to Britain in the conduct of her international relations, but it is important to see them in this light and not as something which stamps Britain and her Commonwealth partners as belonging in some sense to a separate group, which may expect to be treated differently by other countries on account of their special Commonwealth ties. For the fact is, as Sir Robert Hall has recently pointed out, 'that the Commonwealth cannot be an action group in a political sense, because there are not many matters of political importance where the members are all on the same side.'[4]

This comment is equally applicable to strategy and to most economic matters, in which no serious attempt is made nowadays to formulate policies applicable by all or most Commonwealth members. The communiqués following successive conferences of Commonwealth Prime Ministers testify to the truth of this assertion. The joint declaration on disarmament which followed the conference of 1961 is a rare exception and its practical effect upon subsequent disarmament negotiations seems to have been negligible. Probably education is the one important field in which the Commonwealth may be considered as an effective action group, for Commonwealth educational programmes have now gone beyond mere bilateral exchanges between Britain and the rest of the Commonwealth and will no doubt increasingly acquire the character of a multilateral

---

[4] Article in the *Listener*, 13 Feb. 1964, by Sir Robert Hall, Economic Adviser to the British Government, 1953–61, and now Principal of Hertford College, Oxford.

system operating among the whole group of countries. No one would wish to see this process slowed down, and no one would deny its long-term value to all the participants, but it would be wrong to base upon a relationship of this kind an expectation of common policy-making, which it manifestly does not justify.

The truth about Commonwealth membership was well expressed by the late Peter Fraser, the former Prime Minister of New Zealand, when he described it as 'Independence plus'. Independence is of its essence. Again and again it has been repeated by Commonwealth Prime Ministers that membership does not restrict national freedom of action, which of course includes freedom to associate with non-members and to remain unaligned in one another's disputes. The 'plus' element in the relationship is also real, but it is something which a country may hope to add to its other relationships. It is not and cannot be an alternative option or policy.

Because the Commonwealth spans the continents and the races, the ease of communication with one another, which most of its members enjoy, is capable of making a valuable contribution to international understanding. But it should be thought of as a lubricant, which helps to make international co-operation work, not as being itself a significant piece of independent international machinery for getting things done. It is particularly important for Britain herself to see it in this light, for this is how it is already seen by others, including Commonwealth members, all around the world, and any attempt by Britain to institutionalize its traditions and practices or to base distinct policies upon it is doomed to failure. The scope for informal co-operation among Commonwealth countries in the course of normal diplomacy and within the numerous international organizations to which they mostly belong may yet be great. The scope for co-operation among them for the promotion of common action by the Commonwealth as a whole or for purposes in which others do not share is almost nil.

7

Policy for the Future

THE policies which Britain ought now to pursue cannot be reduced to any simple rule of thumb, for the situation which she faces is complex and its evolution is full of imponderables. Nevertheless the argument which has been presented here points fairly clearly to a number of propositions which, if they do not add up to a new policy, at least imply a new national attitude towards the role which Britain should now seek to play. This is well worth establishing, for what a government does in the face of new situations is largely determined by the picture which it has at the time of the place which the country occupies, or should occupy among the nations. Where a country's situation has been changing as fast as Britain's and for so long, it is all too likely that this picture will be constantly somewhat out of date.

The end of an era

The first point to make is that the present period marks with unusual clarity the end of an era in world affairs in which European countries carved most of the world up into areas of special influence and wrangled and fought with one another for positions of power all around the globe as well as in Europe itself. A whole international system was built upon this foundation and now, with astonishing rapidity it has broken up and vanished. It is not being replaced by a similar system run by different powers, but by something new and different, and the birth of the new order, whose precise form cannot yet be clearly seen, is proving to be an uneasy and sometimes a dangerous experience. Britain has been at the centre of this process, because she was at the centre of the old system. Throughout nearly all of this century her foreign policy has been conditioned by old obligations, which it became ever harder to meet in a changing world. 'For more than forty years Britain has been making a strategic retreat', wrote Lord Franks.[1] 'We have had a great deal to retreat from: a position of eminence unchallenged in the nineteenth century world.' On the whole this retreat has been managed with skill and realism. The welfare of the British people has certainly not suffered and it is only in the last few years that some weariness and exasperation at the absence of fresh, new horizons has become apparent. Now, in the few years between about 1957 and 1964, Britain has come virtually to the end of this particular road. What is left of the old tasks is no more than a final tidying up operation and there is now nothing to prevent Britain from looking ahead, unencumbered by the legacy of her remarkable past. The next decade in British policy should therefore be sharply differentiated from the one that is just past, for it is only in our own minds that the old conditions are at all likely to linger on.

The second point which has emerged is the extraordinarily varied nature of Britain's international interests and requirements. These are still world wide, though with the growth of other centres of power and of the interdependence of all areas, the way in which they have to be safeguarded has changed. When Harold Wilson said 'We should not be corralled in Europe', he might have added 'or anywhere else either.' For Britain cannot afford

[1] Article in *Sunday Times*, 26 Apr. 1964.

to be corralled in any sectional group if by 'corralled' one means shut in and deprived of liberty in one's relations with the rest of the world. Certain types of proposals made from time to time in a Commonwealth context could have this effect as surely as integration into the wrong kind of Europe.

For Britain, the widest multilateral relationships in politics, in defence, and in trade are a necessity. She can never be content with the defence of specifically British positions or privileges, but must always be even more deeply concerned with the maintenance of reasonable stability and of open access to trade throughout the world. In the exceptional conditions of the nineteenth century the imperial system was able to achieve both these aims simultaneously and Britain could benefit both from the advantages of direct control over numerous areas and from the maintenance of a wider Pax Britannica. No such combination is practicable today, when the perpetuation of old positions of power usually calls into existence rival forces which threaten the even more important requirement of the maintenance of peace. That is why the withdrawal of imperial power has so often since 1945 proved to be the policy most consistent with security, despite the obvious risk of creating a power vacuum. The reluctant and belated withdrawal of French military power from Indo-China, and the almost equally sluggish reactions of Britain to new situations in the Middle East, both provide instances where the risk of creating a power vacuum was real, but nevertheless proved smaller than the dangers involved in trying to maintain law and order by the old methods.

The concept of multilateralism

What has now to be attempted is the creation of a new multilateral system of a less self-defeating nature than the old one has now become. Although most of the former imperial powers have paid lip-service to this idea, their allegiance to it has in practice been fitful and uncertain, as the Congo crisis showed, because the immediate threat to their sectional interests still continued to take priority in their minds. This mentality not only prolonged the painful period of imperial retreat but has delayed the creation of more up-to-date security techniques, which require the full support of these same powers if they are to be made effective.

If the concept of multilateralism is accepted, the moral for the Commonwealth is clear. It is that, while good relations and expanding trade among member countries are as important as ever, the concept of the Commonwealth as a separate group possessing some distinctive common interest is outdated. This concept has served a useful purpose in the immediate transition from dependence to independence. For Britain, it has reduced the difficulty of relinquishing power. For the other Commonwealth countries, it has eased their entry into international society, especially through their continuing intimacy with an established and experienced world power, Britain. But this is of its very nature a passing interlude in the history of the different Commonwealth countries, and already the most constructive phase of the interlude is nearing its end. For what is now happening throughout the whole group is that each country is searching for a new identity and is inevitably finding it increasingly in relationships to which the Commonwealth as a group is, at best, irrelevant. At worst it may even be an obstacle, if any attempt is made to base defence or economic policies upon it.

The evolution of the attitude of Australia, whose sentimental attachment to the Commonwealth concept has been outstanding, provides a clear illustration of this. As far back as 1951 she was obliged to give formal recognition to the inadequacy of the Commonwealth as a guardian of Australian security by agreeing to British exclusion from the ANZUS pact. Since then, as her population and her economy have expanded, the trends of investment and trade have made it increasingly clear that the essential diversification of Australian interests cannot be expected to take place within a Commonwealth framework, even though trade with some Commonwealth countries, including Britain, continues to be important. 'We are a Pacific and Indian Ocean people', said a leading Australian banker recently.[2] 'We are a part of Asia. Our future lies in the region where we live and where most of the world's people live.' The background against which he spoke included impressive new figures for Australia's trade with the United States, Japan, and Europe, showing that Australia's switch to multilateralism and away from a specifically Commonwealth pattern is at least as striking as Britain's. Similar trends are developing among the more recently independent Commonwealth countries in Africa and elsewhere.

There is therefore no need for Britain to feel any sense of guilt or of abdication of responsibility in seeking a new identity for herself, in which her direct responsibilities to certain of her former dependencies will be diluted by the participation of other powers, or of international organizations or by the growth of local and regional loyalties. These things are inherent in the kaleidoscopic changes which are occurring in the external relations of all Britain's Commonwealth partners just as much as in her

[2] Sir Warren Macdonald, Chairman of the Commonwealth Banking Corporation, speaking in Sydney, 11 May 1964 (*The Times*, 12 May 1964).

own. It is far better to recognize this openly and to plan the necessary adjustments, than to pretend that there is an intention to perpetuate old arrangements long after others have seen the writing on the wall.

The search for international identity

In the search for a new international identity which so many countries, including Britain, are pursuing, regionalism has been playing a growing part. This is a natural result of the break-up of the nineteenth-century pattern, in which the power-lines radiated out from Europe, connecting London with Delhi and Sydney, Paris with Brazzaville and Saigon, The Hague with Jakarta and Brussels with Léopoldville. With the weakening of these links, or at least of their exclusive quality, geography has begun to reassert itself and is causing the countries at both ends of the old colonial lifeline to think more of relations with their neighbours.

No doubt this process will go on, especially since in some of the former colonial areas, such as West Africa, it is only just beginning. Provided that it does not result in a splitting of the world into autarchic regional blocs, inspired by a kind of enlarged nationalism, it is an evolution to which exception cannot be taken in an age when so many of the old nation-states are coming to find their boundaries and resources too restrictive for modern needs. All the same, too much virtue should not be attributed to mere geographical propinquity as a criterion for union. What matters most in the joining together of separate political units is their capacity to do more together than they can do apart. The test, in other words, is whether they can form an 'action group', and geography, though no doubt a convenient ally, is not necessarily decisive. It would indeed be ironical if it came to be so thought of in an age when modern communications have come so near to annihilating distance as a barrier between nations and continents. In any case, so far as Britain is concerned, no action group, whether based mainly on geographical propinquity or on other factors, could be acceptable if membership of it had the effect of cutting her off from those outside. Her purpose in joining would be to secure a more effective base for continued activity in the affairs of the world as a whole, not simply to become more intensely absorbed in the affairs of a single region. It is in this context that her relations with the European continent and the countries of the Atlantic area have to be considered.

The pattern of co-operation

In defence, regionalism is still important, despite the world-wide range of modern missiles. De Gaulle goes so far as to insist that defence is still a matter for the independent nation and he treats NATO accordingly. This seems an unduly old-fashioned view to take in Western Europe, which has become small, not merely in relation to modern weapons of mass destruction but also in relation to modern conventional forces. If defence still has to be maintained, as virtually everybody agrees that it must, then collective defence along with European neighbours and with the only Western country capable of remaining in the first rank of nuclear powers is the obvious system for Britain to support. To say this, and consequently to work for military co-operation between Western Europe and the United States, is not to assume that the danger of massive military attack upon Western Europe has remained exactly as it was when NATO was formed or that it is bound to continue indefinitely. Nor is it to argue for any particular level of military effort by the West, for this must be a matter of judgement from time to time. It is simply to assert that strategic unity in the West is still an asset in dealing with the Soviet Union and other great powers, whether this is thought of primarily as a question of defence and deterrence or as one of negotiation for disarmament and for other peaceful purposes.

Unity among the Western powers is not in any event likely to be monolithic, nor to be equally in evidence all over the world. What is both practicable and sensible is to work for a high degree of common action through NATO in the military defence of the Atlantic area and, for the rest, to seek less formal co-operation, through a wide range of organizations, which are not confined to the so-called Atlantic powers, over the whole range of world problems. This seems at present to be in any case the limit of what is attainable. It may well also be the limit of what is desirable, for any systematic attempt by this particular group of nations to organize their immense economic and military power for the purpose of imposing their collective will throughout the world would be likely to stir up resistances which would make the effort self-defeating. Moreover the system to which the advanced powers of the West should look for their future security is not one in which they exercise world domination, but one in which a number of centres of power can be brought to accept some measure of international authority, at least for the purpose of restricting armed conflict in all its forms and for preventing nuclear war.

In economics, the same countries form the core of the action group with which Britain must co-operate. This is not because they must necessarily be Britain's predominant trading partners, for Britain's trade has been and still is widely diversified. It is rather because they include a high proportion of those non-communist powers, which have economic capacities and needs similar to Britain's. If effective international policies are to be worked out for trade and aid, for investment and finance, it is with these countries above all that common action will have to be agreed. The group is clearly not exclusive. It already includes Japan and will no doubt come increasingly to include other industrializing countries both inside and outside the Commonwealth, but for some time ahead the weight of Europe and North America is likely to remain preponderant when policies come to be threshed out in the GATT, the International Monetary Fund, the World Bank, or elsewhere. For these reasons, rather than on account of mere geographical propinquity, what is done by these countries matters more to Britain than what is done by any other group in the world. To influence them and to prevent them from pulling in opposite directions is therefore a cardinal object of British policy. How best to position herself to exercise this influence was the real question which Britain was seeking to answer by applying to join the European Economic Community. With the failure of the Brussels negotiations, the question still remains open, but it cannot indefinitely remain so.

The optimum solution for Britain would be to obtain whatever advantages may flow from large-scale enterprise based upon a large home market, by joining with those countries which are both her neighbours and her industrial equals to form a community large and powerful enough to hold its own with other giant economies. For this, Britain would have to be prepared for economic, and no doubt eventually political, integration with Europe of an advanced though not yet clearly definable kind. This could be tolerable to her only if she felt reasonably assured that the integrated community, which she was joining, was likely to be 'outward-looking'.

The policies implied by this over-worked but none the less expressive word are varied and far-reaching and can be implemented only by the co-operation of virtually the

I*

whole of the developed industrial world. In particular, a constructive European attitude in these matters is almost equally important to Britain whether she becomes politically integrated with the Continent or not. The policies include co-operation with North America for defence and disarmament and for the settlement of disputes between East and West; they also include joint policies in the field of trade and aid designed to promote development and to narrow the yawning gap between North and South. On these huge issues Britain is manifestly unable to make much impact by herself, yet they are the issues which will determine her future.

To persuade others to co-operate with her and with each other for these purposes is therefore a far greater British interest, to say nothing of the world's interest in it, than to pursue the same aims on her own.

Despite the general confusion within the Western alliance during 1963 and 1964, there is a good chance that European co-operation in the pursuit of these aims can be secured, and there is reason for thinking that Britain's actions can substantially help or hinder the effort to do this. The interests of Britain's neighbours are not essentially different from her own, and many Europeans are themselves convinced of this. In the long run they need the same sort of world as Britain, and even if they join together to form a large unit, a narrowly autarchic Europe is for most of them no more than a second best. The present ambivalence of feeling in Europe, where the issue still hangs in the balance, is in large measure due to a strong reaction, primarily in France but discernible in most other European countries, against the position of exceptional dominance which the United States has enjoyed in their affairs since 1945. This has not been the fault of the United States, but simply a reflection of an unnatural situation, which inevitably gave rise to a sense of humiliation and impotence on the European side. Once European morale had recovered, adjustments in the relationship were bound to be required.

It is unfortunate that this phase should have found at the head of the French government an individual who adds to the general European mood a personal resentment against the United States and a mystical devotion to the concept of the national grandeur of France. This coincidence makes the necessary adjustments harder and more precarious than they need have been, but it does not change the necessity for Europe to find a new and constructive role in an age when world-wide interdependence has become more a condition of existence than a matter of choice. The powerful forces in Europe which understand this and think de Gaulle's brand of Europeanism outdated would respond readily to any modification of the Western alliance system which offered satisfaction to the reasonable demand in Europe for a larger share in its direction. It is here that Britain can make an important contribution if she decides soon enough and clearly enough upon the overall objective which she is trying to achieve.

Policy towards the EEC

The inescapable effect of the breakdown of the Brussels negotiations was to exclude Britain from playing any direct part in the evolution of the Community for a further period. Her numerous friends in the Community, above all the Dutch, resolved to do what they could to keep the door open for her, at least until after the British General Election of 1964 was past, but after that the pressure for some new initiative is bound to grow.

On this Britain faces a genuine dilemma. On the one hand those in Europe who seek British association with the Continent's future cannot work whole-heartedly for this purpose so long as the British attitude to Europe remains ambiguous. On the other hand, so long as there is no change in the French policy which kept Britain out in January 1963, it is difficult for Britain to take a categorical initiative, because it would encounter a swift rebuff from France unless it was accompanied by express acceptance of a number of Gaullist propositions, which a large part of the Community itself is at present engaged in combating.

There is therefore a real danger that Europeans will wait with increasing impatience for a sign from Britain, that the sign will not come, and that Britain will then be written off in the European mind, not only as a future member of the Community but, more generally, as an influence in European affairs. For even the most outward-looking of Europeans is bound in the end to become tired of being more British on Britain's behalf than the British are willing to be European. The one favourable feature in this intrinsically difficult tactical situation is that de Gaulle's attitude towards European integration and the nationalist quality of his foreign policy are by their very nature likely to slow down the tempo at which the Community can evolve the kind of formal institutions which would make eventual British association with Europe harder. There may therefore be sufficient time still left to allow British post-election attitudes to crystallize, to allow the relationship between Europe and North America to be rationally sorted out within NATO, and to allow the underlying strength or weakness of Gaullist ambitions for France to be more confidently assessed.

What is required of Britain, in the limited time now vouchsafed to her, is that she should express, as unequivocally as possible, her acceptance of solidarity with Europe, coupled with a claim to a major voice in European affairs, as the basis of her future policy. There would obviously be no point in giving this the form of a fresh application to join EEC, since at the present time this would be a move which could have no immediately constructive sequel and would therefore be more likely to fragment than to unite opinion both in Europe and in Britain. What is needed is a proposal, in a field where early action is possible, which could be seen to place Britain squarely at the side of her European neighbours on a footing of complete equality.

The obvious and perhaps the only area of policy in which a proposal of this kind now seems practicable is nuclear strategy. Here is a problem which is proving disruptive of Western unity because of the immense gap in power between the United States and all her allies and because of the real difficulty of devising a system which combines concentration of decision in emergency with consultation and the sharing of information in the making of policy. It is a problem in which wrong solutions could both destroy Western unity and complicate, if not frustrate, negotiations with the East over disarmament and arms control. It is therefore a problem about which something must be done and on which several rival trends of thought are now competing for the mastery, as the disputes over the multilateral force and the French refusal to participate in the nuclear test-ban treaty bear witness. Finally, it is a problem to whose solution Britain is unusually well fitted to make a contribution, since she has both something to gain from a satisfactory outcome to the nuclear difficulties of the alliance and also something tangible to offer to others by way of inducement.

What she has to gain is the establishment of a collective system which promises her greater permanence and possibly less economic strain than her present precarious reliance on her own national nuclear effort, dependent as it is upon protracted American support. What she has to offer, especially to France, is a way of escape from a national effort in nuclear armament which, at the present time, seems to threaten France with the prospect of even more alarming economic burdens for even less eventual effectiveness than Britain herself faces. Britain is in a position to offer a way out of this because, by accepting complete equality of status with her European allies in nuclear strategy and by putting her own nuclear forces under an allied command in which they have a voice, she can go far to end the sense of unfair discrimination from which present French policies largely derive. Not least, she is well-placed, as the only beneficiary of special treatment in Washington, to assist in persuading the United States to extend to a wider group, in which Britain would be an equal partner, a sufficient share in the policy-making process, together with whatever technical information may be necessary for the purpose, to ward off the risk that a more dangerous European separatism may develop in the nuclear field.

It may be that a move of this kind by Britain is the only major step of a positive kind which is at present open to her in her relations with Europe. It is advocated here on its own merits as a contribution to the nuclear policies of the West as a whole and in the belief that it would serve British strategic interests better than any other alternative policy. That it would also keep the door open for eventual British participation in Europe's political evolution is a bonus from which future dividends may reasonably be expected. The price to be paid for it in terms of loss of British power of independent action is substantial enough in the short run to enable the gesture to carry conviction in Europe. In the longer run, when the benefits to Britain of the present Nassau agreement have run their course, the British power of independent action does not in any event seem likely to be great and, for that very reason, its value as a bargaining counter will have become severely depreciated.

Other positive steps which Britain might take towards Europe are probably only of a minor character, such as further advances towards standardization in coinage, weights and measures, and the building of cross-Channel highways. In the negative sense, however, there are some attitudes and policies which Britain should consciously avoid.

Multilateralism in practice

Britain should not seek to build exclusive systems or institutions upon her former imperial connexions. This applies to the British role in world security, with its dependence upon overseas military bases. These have lost or are steadily losing their original utility but nevertheless serve to perpetuate Britain's deeply ingrained belief that she has a destiny which separates her from other industrial nations of similar size and power. Britain should not attempt to maintain indefinitely or to develop further the discriminatory features which have characterized Commonwealth trading arrangements in the last thirty years. She should not make a virtue of maintaining the proud separatism of sterling but, as with the ex-imperial bases, she should look for its conversion into a more broadly-supported system. She should not aim to prolong a privileged status among the allies of the United States, except in so far as this may be based upon the bonds of language and culture and the quality of the contribution which she makes to common causes. These abstentions from courses previously followed have already been urged on their individual merits. They would all have the further advantage of easing the transition which Britain has to make in her relations with the European continent. This is not a coincidence, but on the contrary is evidence that Britain's relations with the more distant parts of the world and her relations with her nearest neighbours in Europe, so far from being in conflict with one another, are subject to the same forces which are changing the pattern of power and international relations all over the world.

This catalogue of negatives, of courses which Britain should in future avoid, points the way to the more positive attitude which she must adopt instead. If it be true that her interests in almost every field require increasingly the co-operation of other nations both for security and for trade, then it follows that she should set in the forefront of her policy the organization of international relations in a way which gives to a medium-sized power the widest scope for securing the collective action which meets her needs. Innumerable international agencies already exist for such purposes, some under the United Nations and some not, some regional and some functional, some for economic collaboration and some for defence. Yet it is still true that the largest powers, and those former great powers whose resources no longer place them in the front rank, have not on the whole chosen to use this network of multilateral international bodies to its full capacity but have preferred to rely upon their own resources and traditional diplomacy where their own major interests are at stake. The drive for the development of international organization in its wider forms has, not unnaturally, come from the small and weak, or from the group of lesser medium-sized powers, notably the Scandinavian countries and Canada. The result is that the power and effectiveness of most international organizations has remained limited, except where, like NATO or the GATT, they have seemed to offer to some at least of the most powerful countries the only available way of pursuing certain specific national interests.

The time has now arrived when the interest of some of the larger medium powers, including Britain, points increasingly to the need to use the new multilateral techniques more positively and over a wider range of subjects. Britain, like most of the old powers, has been reluctant to entrust to the uncertainties of multilateral diplomacy situations which she would formerly have handled on her own, an inhibition which has applied particularly to the use of the United Nations. To a certain extent this reluctance has been justified in the past, for Britain has had to conduct a number of delicate operations in the course of her long strategic retreat, which would not have been facilitated by the active intervention of numerous powers which had little knowledge of the problems involved and too often felt little responsibility for their solution. On the whole Britain during this period has shown a good deal of talent in handling these situations herself, in a manner reasonably acceptable to wider international opinion, but without countenancing international intervention.

What makes it both possible and necessary for Britain now to modify her attitude is, firstly, that there will in future be few situations in which Britain will have to negotiate a major constitutional change in bilateral dealings with a dependent territory as she has so often done in the past. From now onwards, not only will it not be necessary for Britain to handle her remaining overseas problems as though they were her domestic concern; it will scarcely ever be possible. International concern for the situation in South Arabia, or in Malaysia, or in the High Commission Territories in Africa or, possibly, in British Guiana or Hong Kong, is quite unavoidable and, more important, action by outside powers, which Britain will be in no position to prevent, will greatly affect the nature of the settlements which it will eventually be possible to make. The time has therefore now come when Britain would be wise to use all the facilities offered by international organizations in order to mobilize from the start the maximum weight of outside opinion and even of outside material participation in the search for solutions of such problems.

In this respect the Cyprus crisis of 1963-4 may, in retrospect, seem like a turning point. Here was a situation in a Commonwealth country, involving conflicting elements which drew in several members of NATO. Yet attempts to deal with it first on a Commonwealth and then on a NATO basis quickly failed, and the matter was placed by the British government in the hands of the United Nations. Ten or even five years earlier British action of this kind would have been scarcely conceivable, nor would it then have seemed likely that British troops could continue to operate in the field under United Nations command.

At the time of writing it is impossible to guess whether, under United Nations auspices, a tolerable solution will be found in Cyprus, but what is already clear is that, by the time the United Nations was called in, every other method had failed. It is also clear that, whatever happens, Britain will have gained substantially from her insistence upon distributing among others some share of the responsibility for a situation which she herself no longer had effective power to control. This in itself is justification for the step which was taken. If, in addition, it forces other leading powers to apply more of their intellectual and material resources to equipping the United Nations for tasks of this kind, the gain will be the greater. In this instance it was, once again, Canada and the Scandinavians who were the first to enable the United Nations operation to get under way, and it was the Canadian Prime Minister who was the first to demand new and better procedures for the future. If Britain were to become effectively associated with such thinking in future and were to use international machinery herself in the early stages of disputes, international action could be brought to a new level of effectiveness.

It is, of course, perfectly true that, in the present state of great power relationships, there will continue to be types of situation in which the United Nations, with its divided counsels, its financial weakness, and its incomplete security machinery, will be an inadequate instrument, but the importance of this can be exaggerated. The situations with which the United Nations cannot deal are, broadly, those where either serious fighting, beyond the scope of a peace-keeping force, becomes necessary or the interests of the great powers are directly involved. Vietnam and Laos have provided examples of the first, Cuba of the second. In both, diplomacy among the major powers and pressures exercised by them are likely to be the determining factors, even if some conciliatory role can also be played by the United Nations. Nevertheless the range of situations in which the great powers are prepared to take risks with each other, or are even willing to confront one another directly by taking sides openly in other people's quarrels, has been steadily narrowing. Various forms of insulating techniques, which may involve United Nations mediation or the appointment of some form of international commission, are coming to be found useful. In any case, the fact that there are undoubtedly some situations where the United Nations cannot operate is no reason for failing to employ it in the growing number of cases where it can.

There has been in recent years, especially after the Suez affair of 1956 and again during the Congo crisis, a feeling of humiliation in some British political circles at the very thought that, in matters where British interests are affected, Britain may have to defer to the opinions of a large and varied group of countries, collected in the General

Assembly of the United Nations or in some other international body, whose collective quality is too readily presumed to be that of an irresponsible mob. As in any other debating body, many foolish things are said in the United Nations as well as wise ones. Often, as in any national parliament, much of what is said is directed more to future aspirations than to existing difficulties, a feature which has been particularly applicable to some of the debates on colonial issues in the past. This is no more catastrophic in the United Nations than it is in the British House of Commons, and the action, if any, which results, is far more closely related to the realities of power and to the willingness of member states to commit their own resources than would appear from a mere reading of the debating record.

In any case Britain, having for centuries had widely varied and scattered interests and often inadequate means of her own with which to protect them, has always been compelled to take more account of international opinion than has been usual with other great powers. As long ago as 1907, at the height of British imperial power, a famous Foreign Office memorandum[3] addressed to the Foreign Secretary, Sir Edward Grey, asserted that danger to Britain's world-wide interests could only be averted on condition that her policy

is so directed as to harmonize, with the general desires and ideas common to all mankind, and more particularly that it is closely identified with the primary and vital interests of a majority, or as many as possible, of the other nations.

In those days there were fewer other nations to consider and there was no international forum to give publicity to

---

[3] 'Memorandum by Mr Eyre Crowe on the Present State of British Relations with France and Germany, Foreign Office, 1 Jan. 1907', in G. P. Gooch and H. Temperley, *British Documents on the Origins of the War, 1898–1911*, iii (1928), p. 402.

their views, but the principle wisely enjoined upon the Foreign Secretary then is still sound. Indeed, it is at least arguable that victory in the present ideological conflict is even more likely now than in the circumstances of 1907 to go to those who manage to harmonize their own policies with 'the ideas common to all mankind'. It would no doubt be Utopian to imagine that this injunction can be followed at all times and in all places. Nevertheless Britain might do worse than to apply this test to her policies and to think well before rejecting it in favour of more pedestrian or parochial considerations.

A new national purpose

A country's policy must be firmly based in the current realities of the world around it and in the pursuit of its essential interests. This much may be conceded, but is it, by itself, enough? 'Much confusion can be averted by thinking of it [British foreign policy]', wrote C. M. Woodhouse,[4] 'in terms of "protecting interests" rather than "pursuing objectives".' Later he wrote[5] of Britain in the 1950s that she 'was not a power that wished to bring about radical changes in the world but to live with the world as it was. British policy . . . is not to achieve objectives but to protect interests.'

One may sympathize with the wish of the historian to discount the often disingenuous pronouncements of statesmen, bent on explaining their countries' essentially self-seeking policies in terms of honour or democracy or peace, and with his desire to reduce moralizing to a minimum. But to eliminate 'objectives' does not serve the purpose, for what a country's interests are at any given time is by no means self-evident, and the varying judgements of men about them is likely to depend at least in part upon vary-

[4] *British Foreign Policy Since the Second World War* (1961), p. 7.
[5] Ibid., p. 244.

ing philosophical, religious, or political views of what the country's objectives are or ought to be. If one wishes to avoid moralizing, one can think of a country's objectives as a long-range view of its interests, but, whichever way it is expressed, the need of the policy-maker to look beyond clearly defined interests to less precise long-term objectives is inescapable. At the very least, if he fails to do this, his chances of mobilizing the efforts of all classes of citizens, even in the defence of what he has chosen to define as national interests, are much reduced. What may be sufficient for the needs of the historian, concerned to dissect and record the past, is therefore inadequate as a guide for the statesman, who is seeking to mould the future.

The sense of having a definable objective is particularly necessary for Britain in the aftermath of Empire, for there is no doubt that British people have for generations been brought up to believe that they were serving not only their own interests but great causes as well, bearing the white man's burden or fighting wars for the defence of democracy and freedom. In each of these beliefs there was a core of truth, even if there was also some self-deception. In each case the sense of purpose evoked much genuine idealism and effort. So far as the Empire was concerned there is, in retrospect, much room for cynicism, but the colonial district officer, sweating in the tropical jungle, was not wrong in thinking that, in the most disinterested sense, he was doing good, and it was largely his conviction that he was furthering a worth-while objective which so often enabled him to maintain a high vocational standard.

These particular objectives are no longer available to us, not because we are lesser men than our fathers but because the world around us has moved on. Are we then to say that British policy today has no objectives, only interests, and that we wish to bring about no radical changes in the world, only to live with it as it is?

One may doubt whether such a formula would be sufficient to extract serious effort, let alone dynamism or sacrifice from any people. Yet these things are certainly going to be demanded of the British people, who have now to modernize themselves technically, commercially, and socially and to adjust themselves to an entirely new position in the world. Unless their task can be presented to them in terms of worth-while objectives, people who have seen the gods they were brought up with crumble and are offered nothing to replace them are more likely to sink into a rather querulous cynicism. 'Nations which have known empire', wrote John Strachey,[6] 'may simply break their hearts if they do not find a higher ideal than personal enrichment by which to live.'

Anyone who thinks that this colourful phrase overstates the popular feeling about Britain's current situation, might reflect on the extraordinary violence of the reaction in the highest political circles when a well-tried American friend of Britain, Dean Acheson, uttered the obvious truth that Britain had lost an empire and had not yet found a role, adding that her attempt to play a separate power role was about played out.[7]

The outburst of indignation which greeted these remarks was evidence enough of an unhealthy sense of humiliation and a reluctance to face realities. A more constructive response would be to offer to the British people a fresh overall objective, which might help to explain and justify the day-to-day calls which are likely to be made upon them and which can be seen to be relevant both to the position of British interests and to the promotion of a secure and prosperous international order in the future.

[6] *The End of Empire* (1959), p. 229.
[7] Speech by Dean Acheson at the U.S. Military Academy, West Point, 5 Dec. 1962 (USIS, 7 Dec. 1962).

The objective must, of course, necessarily be a national one, in the sense that it must describe a purpose which it will be for the British people in their national community to pursue. But it has been a theme of this book that the objective cannot be national in its substance, nor can it be confined to any one group of countries, whether based on geography like Europe or on history like the Commonwealth. To be satisfying, the objectives must harmonize reasonably with interests and since, as has been argued, Britain's interests are world-wide, her objectives must be world-wide too. On this level Britain does wish for radical changes, not changes in frontiers or in national spheres of influence, but in the global organization both of military security and of the war against backwardness and poverty.

It may be objected that to formulate the national purpose in terms both so broad and so long-range as this is to deprive it of the practical quality which alone can give it force. But this need not be so, for there are always available, in the international organization of security and trade and aid, many things for governments to do, which they are more likely to do consistently and well if they see them as steps towards a wider eventual goal. That pragmatism can be combined with a powerful drive towards a long-term objective was never better illustrated than by the example of Dag Hammarskjöld, the most effective international organizer of his time. In discussing the possibility of world federalism, he wrote:[8]

> I think it is wise to avoid talking of this or that kind of ultimate political target and to realize that the development is still in an early stage of institutional evolution, although a few vanguard penetrations into the constitutional area have taken place. What seems imperative is to push forward institutionally and, eventually, constitutionally all along the line,

[8] Carnegie Endowment for International Peace, *Perspectives on Peace, 1910–1960* (1960), p. 68.

guided by current needs and experiences, without preconceived ideas of the ultimate form.

No one could accuse Dag Hammarskjöld of not having an overall objective to which all his day-to-day efforts were directed. Yet this passage showed, as his performance in office showed, that he was as responsive to the immediate realities of power and sectional interests as any national politician. What distinguished him and gave his work its force was his unusually clear concept of where he was trying to go in building a more humane and stable international order.

If an objective of this kind were clearly formulated and its practical reality emphasized by consistent government policies, pursued both through international organizations and through normal diplomacy, there would be no need for British people to 'break their hearts' or to feel that they had today a role any less creditable or exciting than their fathers had before them.